I0437728

THINK SMART, TALK SMART

THINK SMART, TALK SMART

How Scientists Think:
A Guide to Effective Communication

ALLAN LAURENCE BROOKS

THINK SMART, TALK SMART
HOW SCIENTISTS THINK:
A GUIDE TO EFFECTIVE COMMUNICATION

Copyright © 2011 by Allan Laurence Brooks.

All rights reserved. No part of this book may be used or reproduced by any means, graphic, electronic, or mechanical, including photocopying, recording, taping or by any information storage retrieval system without the written permission of the author except in the case of brief quotations embodied in critical articles and reviews.

iUniverse books may be ordered through booksellers or by contacting:

iUniverse
1663 Liberty Drive
Bloomington, IN 47403
www.iuniverse.com
1-800-Authors (1-800-288-4677)

Because of the dynamic nature of the Internet, any web addresses or links contained in this book may have changed since publication and may no longer be valid. The views expressed in this work are solely those of the author and do not necessarily reflect the views of the publisher, and the publisher hereby disclaims any responsibility for them.

Any people depicted in stock imagery provided by Thinkstock are models, and such images are being used for illustrative purposes only.
Certain stock imagery © Thinkstock.

ISBN: 978-1-4620-5847-1 (sc)
ISBN: 978-1-4620-5849-5 (hc)
ISBN: 978-1-4620-5848-8 (e)

Library of Congress Control Number: 2012921236

Print information available on the last page.

iUniverse rev. date: 07/17/2017

CONTENTS

LIST OF ILLUSTRATIONS

PREFACE

Why have I written *Think Smart, Talk Smart*, and why do I ask you to accept the challenges of the title? The chapters presented here deal with two basic human behaviors: communication and thinking. Both are so fundamental that we usually take them for granted. We engage in them intuitively and with little effort, for the most part. Yet what we say and write depends, in large part, on how we think about what's behind those statements. We are usually unaware of our assumptions, premises, and biases and how they affect what we talk about. Too often, what we hope to convey is handled less appropriately or efficiently than necessary to bring about mutual understanding, which leads to effective, mutually agreed-upon action.

I have forty-five years of experience as a graduate engineer, have a Master of Arts in Communication Arts, and have over fifteen years of teaching communications. I have participated in many adult discussion groups and currently lead one. These groups have included mostly college-educated people, many with advanced degrees. These experiences—apart from listening to politicians, talk-show hosts, and guests, among others—have convinced me that we can all benefit from consistent practice of the principles discussed in the following chapters. Sadly, I think, the way ideas are expressed too often reflects the failure of educators to inculcate these principles of critical thinking directly and proactively at all grade levels.

Opening these matters to view can sensitize us and heighten our awareness. I feel that you can use this information as a guide to make sound evaluations, organize your communication, and thus make yourself more effective. (I do not deal here with many aspects of communication, such as grammar, style, etc.)

The things I say may seem obvious after they have been pointed out, but so often we aren't aware of them enough to avoid misinterpretations. I, too, fall into these human lapses in the hustle and bustle of ordinary conversation.

My paragon for the system of communication that combines the inputs of thought with the outputs of expression is the thinking mode of science, so I have a dual purpose in writing this book: One deals with communication, the other is to convey an understanding of essentially what science is.

Finally, a word about a very practical use of language that has contemporary relevance. My use of the masculine pronoun is by no means intended to ignore the feminine half of humankind. Language constantly changes, though basically not with the speed of change of what it must express. As such, we don't yet have a convenient word in all the necessary forms to refer to both sexes in the singular; the use of the plural can sometimes lead to circumlocutions. Please forgive me if I haven't always used the feminine pronoun.

INTRODUCTION

I bet what comes to mind when most people think of science is a vision of white lab coats, test tubes, microscopes, hard-to-grasp theories and mathematical formulae, and today's astonishing technology. All of that, however, is the result of the application of a pattern of thought, which involves the way the scientist seeks understanding and puts observations together. To think smart implies this distinctive style. How scientists think affects the way we form our evaluations.

So, too, the way we talk about our ideas ought to be smart in terms of being meaningful and effective. This does not mean that our *speech* would be any less easy-flowing than our usual style, nor does it imply that the way we speak would be stilted or complex.

I aim to show that my two purposes—talking about communication skills and about science—are not disparate or unrelated but are two edges of a sword that will clear away the underbrush of misunderstanding. Effective communication means effective thinking, and that is the essence of good science.

My approach is pragmatic, with principles illustrated in terms of everyday life. Talking about contemporary events involves the risk of becoming dated, but those that are cited are considered to be of long-lasting significance, typical of others that are apt to occur in the future. They have parallels on a scale from the intrapersonal (our innermost thoughts) to the interpersonal and inter-group, and there are parallels as far up as the international.

Since many of the aspects discussed are interrelated, there may be repetitions and digressions. If one were to describe a tree, one could start with the trunk, follow one large branch, and then one of its smaller branches to some twig. Or if one talked about the major limbs first, one would have to backtrack to deal with the various levels of smaller branches. Another way to look at this is to consider a many-sided polygon, where each vertex is connected to every other vertex. That would make quite a tangle, but I have tried to lead you through the main paths. I will talk about our outputs first—the most apparent aspects of communication. Then I will discuss the inputs, which are acting behind the scenes and are so often unrealized. I intend to stimulate thinking and to be provocative rather than definitive, as the subject is very diffuse.

This should be thought of as a "systems approach," where all aspects affect one another. This is a way of viewing situations, which, as Marshall McLuhan has pointed out, is succeeding the linear, print-related way of looking at the world. It is consistent with contemporary holistic thinking. Such a view is in keeping with the approach to life of people in what we used to call "the Far East." Despite the incompletely quoted line from Kipling, it is most certainly meeting that of the West on an equal footing in an age of jet travel and the Internet.

In our era, when knowledge and diverse subjects have vastly increased over what the Renaissance Man could know, very few of us can be anything but dilettantes in more than one subject. Unless we are scholars or pioneers, so much of our knowledge is received second—or third-hand. I do not pretend to be an expert in many of the topics touched upon in this book. Rather, I speak from training, experience, and intuition. Where my thoughts seem to reflect those of famous people, it does not mean that I have read their works exhaustively. Rather, it indicates how a person of ordinary intelligence can share in the discernment of situations, trends, and relationships that others have pondered.

PART I

OUTPUTS

CHAPTER 1

In the Background

Why should communication be any different for the twenty-first century than it has been in the recent past? Language changes slowly over time, but in any period not everyone is adept at using it. Still, we take our ability to communicate with one another for granted as though it were immutable, requiring little attention. We may be unaware or uncaring about ineffective communication habits. Yet these can get in the way of interpersonal relationships, even inter-group relationships, which provide a practical reason at any time for improving our skills.

Much has happened, though, in the last half of the twentieth century to make improving the effectiveness of communication appropriate, even necessary—that is, getting *through* to people by what we say and how we say it, rather than simply getting *to* them by the way we transmit it. These skills go beyond grammar, which we all hated to study in school; they go beyond vocabulary, which can be accumulated or improved; and they go beyond style of word usage and phraseology, which can depend upon linguistic background, education, and personal characteristics.

The skills I refer to involve the way our communication reflects the way we think. They involve a mindset that is sorely needed to keep up with the pace and demands of the twenty-first century. Think of all that has happened in the past one hundred years!

Globalization is one obvious change. The jet plane, the credit card, and the internationalization of corporations have brought peoples and nations of diverse languages and cultures into intimate contact with one another. In the mid-twentieth century, the United Nations pointed out the need for simultaneous translation, but even that capability did not prevent misunderstanding because of subtleties of word meanings and tones of expression. Diplomatic language can veil ambiguity on purpose, but business communication between different languages needs to be unambiguous to be effective.

3

Electronic technology has almost exploded with possibilities. The Internet is the most recent example that brings diverse people together, as well as friends who may be reached by cell phone. Using the speed of light, it epitomizes the instantaneity with which information can be transmitted. This implies that the chance—or risk—of acting on the information can become even more critical than when a telephone "hot line" was set up between the Soviet Union and the United States during the Cold War. Other frontiers have been breached: electronic voice and facial recognition, artificial translation, even artificial intelligence, for example.

The computer has allowed investigation of several variables at once. Statistics, as will be seen in Chapter 13, has become very sophisticated as a mathematical tool to check the validity of information from scientific research and from public opinion polls. The computer facilitates the use of statistics and helps to speed up even more research.

Information has exploded. With all of the easily observable aspects of nature already investigated, the most hidden ones are now the subjects of PhD dissertations. Since World War II, achieving a doctoral degree has become the minimum requirement for many professions. So we came to the "publish or perish" era. There is such a proliferation of information that it is now often said that today the key to power is information.

With every type of organization flooding us with brochures and blandishments, "junk mail" and telemarketing have brought us to an era of information pollution. What does this say about the significance of the content of what is published? What does it say about our ability to absorb the information and savor its subtleties? It says we need to burnish this wonderful tool of language and our skills in using it.

Finally, *communication* as a subject that has blossomed into a specific discipline, treated as a science. More will be said about this in later chapters, but first, more fundamental advances must be noted.

Two Science Giants

Early in the twentieth century, two powerful scientific concepts were enunciated from the realm of Physics, and they are germane to our subject. How could such seemingly unrelated subjects, such as physics, communication, and making judgments, be related? This will become apparent. Although each concept deals with the most arcane aspects of science, and although each concerns opposite ends of the spatial scale, their implications have helped to shape the way we size up our world.

The two concepts are Einstein's Relativity Theory and Heisenberg's Uncertainty Principle. Don't be terrified by them! One needn't get technical to see how they play a part in effective communication.

As to Relativity, many of us have had experiences that demonstrate in a simple way what Einstein was essentially saying. If a person is on a moving train, and a train on an adjacent track is going in the opposite direction, one cannot tell, apart from feeling the motion, whether the train you are on is standing still and the other one is going backward, or whether the adjacent train is standing still and yours is going forward. Einstein pointed out that while we on Earth consider ourselves to be on a stable, fixed platform, when one gets into outer space, where all the heavenly bodies are in motion, it is impossible to measure exactly where any body is relative to some fixed reference point. Thus, in space, all positions are relative.

Furthermore, because measurements in space depend on light (or other electromagnetic radiations) and because light is dependent on its speed, time is a major determinant in measuring distance in space. So, the second powerful change in conceptualization that Einstein introduced was that time and space are interrelated; they are opposite sides of the same coin.

Apart from this powerful and fundamental way of thinking about concepts that we on Earth tend to give absolute values to, the aspect of this conceptualization that is even more relevant to the way we form evaluations is Einstein's very mode of thinking. This was unique in four respects: One was the way he conceived abstractions; second was the non-absolute nature of these concepts (both of these will be covered in Chapter 12); third was their interrelationships; and fourth, the implication that such concepts depend upon eternal motion and change.

Coming down to earth, what these modes of thinking translate to are the questions we ought to ask ourselves when we talk about abstractions. What do we really mean by "terrorism," "family values," "free enterprise"? How do we measure these ideas? How fixed are our views about them, and therefore how certain can we be of our assessments of them at any one time?

Take the idea of cause and effect, for example. Think how many interpersonal arguments revolve around one party blaming the other for causing a problem. Think how this is scaled up to the arguments between nations. Can a cause be considered in isolation? Is it not the effect of a prior cause that we need to seek? Was the cause perceived at a given time really the source of a problem at the time it was introduced?

And is not our assessment of "the cause" interrelated with many other factors? Was the collapse of the World Trade Center towers the airplanes that crashed into them, an inherent weakness in their structural design, or a Jihad by some terrorists? Was the crash of the American Airlines plane in November 2001 the result of the pilot's overuse of the rudder to control the craft when it encountered turbulence, that disturbance in itself, or a weakness in that plane's design? The tendency is to look for the major cause when most problems result from both a prior condition and an activating event. The tendency to engage in the blame game is like little children claiming, "No, you started it!"

Think, too, of how we characterize people and events with adjectives. We may say someone is clumsy or intelligent, or that an event is disgusting or marvelous. We do so only with implicit and subjective bases for comparison. But such terms cannot be calibrated as scientists do with their instruments.

Scientists have definitive standards for their technical terms. But even with the dictionary, how standard are our definitions? Connotations may change as language changes, however slowly. More importantly, what standards can we have for our evaluations, which frequently involve these connotations as well as imprecise, abstract ideas? Scientific terms are defined operationally. That is, what does the term mean in action, what does the concept do?[1]

---

[1]   For example, "mass" is defined this way: "The property of a body by which it requires force to change its state is called inertia, and mass is the numerical measure of this property." (Handbook of Physics, 2nd ed., in "Dynamical Properties,: E. U. Condon).

This mode of thought is a model to emulate to avoid evaluating poorly.

Einstein's ideas about space and time can be said to imply an indeterminacy of location. At the other end of the physical world, in quantum physics, Werner Heisenberg concluded that if one could determine the position of a subatomic particle within the atom, one could not determine its motion (related to its energy), or, conversely, determining its motion would not allow one to locate its position at any instant. This is almost like viewing a motion picture, where an individual frame cannot be discerned, or, if one sees the latter, one cannot see the motion. More important for its relevance to communication, however, was Heisenberg's realization that the mere act of observing or trying to measure such a particle would affect its properties. This is essentially because the means needed to make such measurements are of the same order of magnitude as the thing measured. One needs a finer tool to measure something coarser.

An example from ordinary life is the way phrasing a question can affect the answer. If a teacher is asked, "Do you feel minority students are underachievers?" the question has two built-in biases, which would be absent if the teacher were asked, "What factors play a part in student achievement?"

Political polls are notorious for slanting the questions so as to produce results that the poll-taking organization favors. We may engage in this sort of manipulation unconsciously and innocently in casual conversation. A woman, with a beaming smile, may ask a friend, "How do you like my new dress?" thus encouraging approval. Instinctively, we all know that our demeanor can affect another person's behavior toward us.

Indeterminacy, as most of us know, is an aspect of normal life. Some of us cope better with such uncertainty than others. Religious people may placate themselves by a belief in God, whom they say "moves in mysterious ways." Or they may accept that, "It is not up to man to answer these questions." In assessing a situation or a problem, such people may accept troublesome aspects or may not take any action to try to change. A more scientific mindset would undoubtedly take either of two paths: either ferret out evidence and try to reason through alternatives to possible solutions, or, with presently imponderable questions such as "What's beyond the Universe?" or "What was there before the Big Bang?" the indeterminacy would be accepted precisely because there is no evidence for an answer. Scientists may certainly believe in God in a spiritual sense, but it is unlikely that most scientists would hold that there is a Being "up there" who plans and controls everything. The reason is that the religious view of God is not based on evidence, certainly not on universally accepted evidence of the same kind. Nor is what some might consider "evidence" independently and consistently reproducible as is required to be the case with scientific experiments.

Acceptance of indeterminacy and awareness of tolerances are not simply mechanical aspects of the scientists' mode of thought; they are psychological aspects of a mindset. That is, while a scientist may have a gnawing dissatisfaction because he or she has not found an explanation for some phenomenon, this is an intellectual challenge; it is not the same kind of troubling anxiety that leads many people to jump to conclusions with erroneous evaluations about vexing problems for which they don't know the cause and can't work out a cure.

Two Others of Note

Two other thinkers of the past century grappled with questions that have to do with communication and judgments. One question arose from the "language of science," mathematics; the other grew from statements about logical propositions.

In the latter part of the nineteenth century, theoretical mathematicians—off in their recondite realm—began to ponder a vexing problem: How could they be sure that the axioms, the bottom-line assumptions upon which they based their reasoning, could be valid for all future theorizing? Could one draw an inference from some axiom that would be inconsistent with another inference that could be drawn from that same axiom? These aspects of validity and consistency hover over all scientific theorizing and are important considerations for opinion forming by the average layman.

In 1914, Kurt Goedel concluded that it would be impossible ever to prove that a set of axioms could be both complete and consistent. If they were complete—that is, for all possible cases—they could not be consistent, and vice versa. This theorem was almost a parallel in logic for Heisenberg's principle. Undoubtedly, this may seem like airy philosophizing, but it had some very basic results: enunciation of the logical rules by which even the axioms were formulated. These were expressed in symbolic logic with signs representing "if," "and," "if this, then . . . ," and other elements that tie statements together.

Even these expressions have to be described at some point by words. Early in the last century, Ludwig Wittgenstein pondered the question of how one could state something in the simplest, most basic, unambiguous manner, such that each word would be intuitively understood without requiring further definition. How could one state the most elemental truth in words? Since language is needed to explore language, we run into the same measurement problem that Heisenberg pointed out. The system couldn't be evaluated by the rules of that system; one couldn't be both judge and juror. Wittgenstein's speculations about the word-as-linguistic-element versus the word-as-indicator led to his claim that the truth of a proposition depends on its verifiability, not on logical thinking alone. Evidence and operational definition strike again! Wittgenstein's work heightened the interest of linguistics, philosophers, and writers in general about the significance of what we say and how we say it.

Communication as a Science

So what qualifies the study of how we talk and think as a science? We think of the latter as a matter of test tubes and microscopes, or more loftily as a pursuit of finding out what makes things tick or as a curiosity about the unknown. Science means orderly experimentation and verification of results. More fundamentally, it is a *mode of thought.* As to how this subject became a science, first, some history.

Toward the end of the nineteenth century, linguistics became a subject of study, particularly in the United States regarding Native American language. Psychology, too, developed as a formal discipline, with studies of how people perceived things, optically and mentally. After World War II, the dynamics of group interactions became a sub-discipline. More recently, the dynamics of resolving conflicts have been explored. That has a most practical goal of communication between individuals and between groups as large as nations. With Nazi propaganda techniques as a goad, the study of persuasion techniques became another sub-discipline. Even subtle behaviors, such as body language, personal space, and movement of eye pupils, became the bases for research as aspects of communication.

Unrealized but underlying all of these aspects is the premise of science. This mode of thought and its protocols of application provide the warp and woof on which we weave the tapestry of virtually every aspect of life today. So, a few words will be said about what this, too, involves.

The minimum requirement is *observation*. This might seem obvious, but it is not so simple. It implies not merely acuteness of what is seen or heard, but an avoidance of selectively choosing what one observes. Furthermore, one observation will not suffice. In order to have significance, duplication is necessary.

Even though scientific instruments are constantly improved to increase precision of observation, the scientific mindset accepts that the data obtained may not have an absolute value. Data have *tolerances* of plus or minus a certain amount. These depend upon the quality of the instrument and the limitations of human observation. Measurements also depend on comparisons with *standards* against which instruments, materials, and processes are calibrated.

Consideration of any observation involves its relationship to its *context* of time and place and to other similar or contrary observations.

Scientists know, too, that it is not sufficient to say that there is no evidence of something, as evidence could be lost, inadequately sought, or destroyed. More basically, it is always possible that somewhere in the universe at some time something might occur or exist. So scientists cannot prove that something does *not* exist, but they can *dis*prove (by obtaining evidence) that something *does* exist. This is referred to as the Null Hypothesis.

Whereas a person who didn't have a scientific bent might take an observation as merely an interesting fact, scientists almost automatically look for a *cause*. That would lead to a tentative idea, a hypothesis, to be followed up by repeated experiments. These aim to show the validity of the idea by preferably using different methods to demonstrate that the idea can be achieved in several ways.

Open-mindedness is needed in all of this. Even though a researcher might have his or her heart set on supporting his own convictions, the true scientific mindset must be dogged but not dogmatic. There is awareness that every cause is the effect of a prior cause and that the process goes on endlessly.

As we all do, the scientist makes inferences about what is probably going on. The difference between what a layman does and what a person with scientific training does is a matter of degree and correctness. The scientist's inferences will be subject to test at some point. In developing concepts about what he or she infers, the ideas have to be traceable to reality. This need not be anything tangible, but it has to at least be grounded in nature. A scientist cannot develop abstract theories out of thin air; these have to grow from a long series of well-established precedents.

It is this dependence on evidence that characterizes the *inductive* nature of scientific thinking. Unlike abstract conclusions that laymen are apt to draw, the concepts of the scientist cannot be based on metaphysics. Similarly, scientists don't start with pre-conceived notions to which they try to fit the facts; that style of thought is *de*ductive and is primarily associated with religious concepts. Even though we are required to conform our behavior to pre-established laws, the latter were developed from experience, that is, inductively.

Observation and hypothesis in science are always open to formal challenge. *Review by one's peers* is required even before and certainly after ideas are published. The scientific temperament has to be one that can accept this, again demonstrating an attitude of openness.

All of the above implies another facet of scientists' awareness: *tentativeness.* The often elusive nature of facts, the acceptance of tolerances, submission to peer review, and the very method of making hypotheses may be understood loosely by most people. Life involves uncertainty. So why do we need Einstein or Heisenberg to tell us this?

My purposes in outlining what these scientists enunciated are several. For one thing, I mean to indicate the type of thinking that scientists possess. I feel it is important to point this out because such thinking is so fundamental and productive to the world today. The realm of communication and evaluation is part of that science. Finally, the specific concepts about relativism, non-absolutism, uncertainty, and the effects of measuring on the measured filter down through philosophers, thinkers, writers, and commentators into the general world view.

Einstein reminds us that in situations that we unconsciously think of as "at rest," the view and the viewer are always changing. Heisenberg teaches us to evaluate our observations in terms of the part we may play in shaping them. Thus we are induced to think of process rather than product, to think of relationships rather than dogmatic acceptance of absolutes. In short, we are urged to be open-minded. So these scientists' views form a framework into which other speculations are placed, and they emphasize points of view that we might merely have taken for granted or have not even thought about.

This is not to say that we ought to communicate in the dry style that scientists are known to use. Nor does it mean that we have to have the same ideas or even the same premises of a scientist or of one another. I do mean, however, that we all ought to come to share the attitude and skills of probity into our ideas and premises and the clarity of communication for which scientists' habits of mind are a model. For today we have a plethora of information, but a dearth of understand among groups of people and frequently between individuals. A more rigorous basis than we have had till now for the exchange of opinions, assessments, and how they came about seems to be called for.

In the chapters that follow, we will look more closely at the way these viewpoints are reflected in particular aspects of our communicative and evaluative behaviors.

CHAPTER 2

Getting Specific:
Conversation, the Rickety Structure

hat is the most critical output of our communications? When we give someone routine information, such as the way we feel, what movie we intend to see, or what we need at the supermarket, these are relatively direct, simple things to say. They usually don't involve a lot of thought or planning nor do they have serious consequences. But how about the opinions and ideas we express? These obviously depend upon many inputs that we have received over long periods of time, absorbed unconsciously from our earliest years and consciously as we grow up. The way we hold these ideas may vary from a gut feeling to a more conscious delineation of them, and the way we express these opinions will depend in part on the extent of that grasp. Our evaluations and opinions are like the foundation of a house, and the communication that expresses these ideas is like the structure of the house itself.

Scientists try to build a firm foundation and then construct a sturdy structure. In this, they are not different from anyone who hopes to offer sound ideas. The scientists' disciplines of thought may be more discriminating in mixing the materials for the foundation, and they may be more exacting in building the structure. If we are to use their mental habits as a model, it behooves us to unravel discrete aspects of a problem and to clarify our own ideas for our own benefit as well as for whatever purpose we put to them. In short, it pays to be specific.

Let's start with a few home-y examples. Think of the wife, busily fixing dinner, who says to her husband, "Get me that bowl in the cupboard." Hubby says, "I don't know what you mean." His wife replies, "You know, the blue one. I need it for this." Husband, wanting to finish reading the sports page, retorts, "How the devil do I know what you're talking about!" This couple may be in for trouble. Then, there is the lady of the house who tells her handyman to "prune the hedges this week." She later complains to him that he has practically denuded the shrubs and decides not to hire him again.

Or consider the factory foreman, who tells his floor boy, "Get those chemicals away from the furnace. They're not safe there." Without telling the floor boy where to put them, he later finds the chemicals stacked in an equally unsafe place and bawls out the floor boy.

These typical examples may seem inconsequential, but they illustrate the little annoyances that matter to the people involved and that can clutter up our days with tension. In each case, the person making the request wasn't clear and the respondent didn't ask. The interpersonal problem could have been avoided if both parties had thought in terms of being specific. They fired off their request with the randomness of a blunderbuss instead of the sharpness of a rifle.

Often, cases may be more diffuse, and evaluations more difficult. If a person goes to a psychotherapist because he feels depressed or if a patient explains that "I have a pain right here," the therapist or the doctor, both trained with a scientific mindset, have to coax from the patient the specifics of such feelings that would be too tedious to mention in casual comments to a friend. The skein of these problems has to be unraveled thread by thread. A person who thinks analytically can see the specific details in relation to one another and group them appropriately (a process called factor analysis) so as to develop an overall picture.

The examples above are given from the viewpoint of the sender of information. He or she may unthinkingly leave it to the receiver to unravel his or her remarks. Suppose we are the receivers, though. How do we unravel what is sent to us? A political candidate may say something like, "We must build this nation strong again. I promise to work for economic gains so that we can protect the health and welfare of everyone." Another politician my say of his opponent, "On his watch, educational levels went down, and school construction lagged."

We're all familiar with these types of remarks, but how do we evaluate them? What is meant by "strong," "economic gains," "health and welfare"? And what is meant by "educational levels" and the "lag" in school construction? The average citizen probably responds to these kinds of remarks with some cynicism, some laziness, and perhaps some awareness of the speaker's record. We can't all be tuned in to all of the important details of every subject that might affect us. However, experience suggests that most people do not say, "Show me the specifics."

That this carelessness can exist in the minds of people who should know better can be shown in giving instructions. Forget the way a housewife may relay a recipe to a friend, or the way one may lead a person astray with driving instructions from the airport to his house. In the business world, instructions sometimes bear this out. One example is seen in a government complaint to a manufacturer of army helmets that his product did not conform to specifications. The manufacturer replied that it was a question of how one interpreted the specifications. Similarly, executives of the company that built the rocket seals that failed in the Challenger disaster claimed that the specifications for the seals were confusing. A systematic mindset that would avoid this problem would adopt the oath a witness takes in a court case. The language of the oath, so robust that it has existed in the same form since the fifteenth century, covers all bases. It's like a boxer knocking out a falsehood with a left and a right. First, it asks, "Do you promise to tell the truth?" Well, that's basic, but it's not enough. Then it comes in with a left punch, asking for sufficiency: "Do you promise to tell the whole truth . . ." Finally, the right hook, preventing unnecessary statements, "and noting but the truth?" Did the political candidate give all of the facts behind his opponent's record on school construction?

Sad to say, most of us haven't been trained to follow this injunction automatically. One of the commissioners of the Rogers Committee investigating the 1986 Challenger disaster said, "People . . . didn't come forth. They downplayed the importance of the seals' resiliency in cold weather, and they raised all sorts of possibilities that they must have known were spurious."[2]

Many habits of mind are involved here, of course: care, patience, discernment, assiduousness, analytic ability. Our minds may be on other important things or we may be insensitive to how we are getting through to other people.

---

[2]   "Record Shows NASA Told of Doubts on Seals," David E. Langer, *New York Time*, August 7,1986

The Journalists' Rule

A useful habit to get into when trying to evaluate a situation is to think of the five W's and the one H that journalists are taught to ask themselves: who, what, when, where, why, and how.

Who can be fairly straightforward, provided one thinks of all the people pertinently involved, directly or indirectly. *What* can refer to situations, events, or objects.

When can be more complex. Time may be judged by the calendar, clock, or descriptive terms, but it also must be considered from the standpoint of duration, which must be broken down into intervals of activity and inactivity. Either of these may occur randomly or evenly, as, for example, with an employee's lateness or absence or a legislator's votes or speeches. Speed, its change and rate of change, and rate of acceleration or slowing down, could also be meaningful, as with political storm clouds gathering or changes in the economy. *When* factors in trends or the unfolding of event

Where can refer to geography or any location, such as that cupboard the housewife sent her husband to. *Why* may be asking for a cause or a purpose, and *how* may refer to the way things work past, present, or future.

One also has to get into the habit of thinking in terms not merely of accuracy but of precision. An archer is accurate if his arrow comes close to the bull's eye in several shots, but he is precise if his aim lands his arrows almost on top of one another within the black, center circle itself. Scientists aim for precision in many ways: In their definitions of terms, in calibration of instruments, in written standards, in the titles of technical and scholarly articles, and by stating the tolerances on their data or calculations. Some of these will be discussed in later chapters.

In a standard dictionary, English is the most prolific and useful language on Earth, giving us plenty of choices for precision. Looking through a thesaurus can be great fun for expanding one's vocabulary.

The Snare of Multiple Meanings

The dictionary would have to be much larger if we didn't have some words where any one by itself could have totally different meanings. Psycholinguists point out that most people don't often immediately detect the alternative meanings for ambiguities. Take the word "bat," for example. That's simple enough by itself to indicate a flying rodent or a baseball bat. But context might condition the meaning. If we said, "The boys found a bat," one might more readily think of baseball bat, as the stereotypical girl might not want to conjure up the icky flying critter! The meaning might depend on whether we said the bat was found in a park or in a cave. Suppose, however, we heard that the boys found a bat in the cave in the park. Perhaps while playing baseball, a rain shower forced them to flee with their gear into a nearby cave. But what did they find?

Some other examples: A consumer affairs inspector at a fish market reports that "The scales look peculiar." The weighing scales or the fish scales? A marketing vice president tells his sales staff, "I want lots of that size." Does he mean numerical lots or merely a large quantity? This type of ambiguity depends on the word alone, so it is called a "lexical ambiguity." The examples may seem ridiculous, but they do occur and can lead to major headaches.

The tendency to jump to conclusions can get us into trouble, especially when the type of ambiguity is more complicated. For example, if a friend reports that she saw the fat doctor's wife in the waiting room, was she referring to a particular doctor in that group or to the wife? Again: If someone said, "People were disturbed by Jones's behavior at the office party," did Jones really behave badly at the office party, or were the people at the office party discussing his prior behavior, whatever it was? These "surface structure ambiguities" depend on the juxtaposition of words.

A more complex type of ambiguity depends on the "deep structure" of the sentence. For example, a husband may tell his wife that he is bored by visiting relatives. The wife's reaction might be sympathetic if she thought her husband simply didn't want to pay a visit. But she might be annoyed if she interpreted his remark to mean that he found the relatives boring. In the statement, "Italians like Americans as much as Germans," do the Italians and Germans equally like Americans, or is it the Italians who are doing the liking? In these last two examples, one way of interpreting the remark would be to have the husband or the Germans act as the subject of the verb, even if implied; in the other meaning, the husband or the Germans would be the objects of the verb.

There may also be an ambiguous interpretation regardless of any of these lexical surface or deep-structure types. At the international level, a classic example with serious consequences occurred during the Cold War in the 1980s when the Reagan administration wanted to develop the "Star Wars" program in space. The Soviet Union, America's adversary at the time, held that the word *current* relating to the state of technology referred to the state of research at the time the treaty was written. The United States, wishing to develop the technology, claimed that *current* referred to the state of research at the time they were making the "Star Wars" request.

Finally, this needs to be mentioned. We're taught in grade school to distinguish between *can* and *may*, regarding permission. If the boss tells you, "You can't make a mistake," is he reassuring you or warning you? Similarly, *must* and *should* can also cause trouble. If your boss says, "You should (or must) know that that's not the way to do that," is he telling you that you should already know this, or that it is your obligation to know? The former could be a reprimand, the latter an instruction. Also, "I'm supposed to be there" can mean that people think you're there already or that you ought to be there in the near future.

What Scientists Do

Scientists, of course, are fortunate to have the language of mathematics to provide precision. While the number 2 might be accurate, precision would require that it be stated at least as 2.0. Depending on the precision required—if accompanying data were given to three decimal places, for example—one would have to say something like 2.067 or, better yet, 2.070 to imply that the 7 was not simply rounded off from 69. This would avoid ambiguity of value.

This becomes a problem when we want to quantify adjectives or adverbs. All we have in English are words like *very*, which we can repeat for emphasis, or *extremely*. We approach the scientists' lingo when we say something like, "On a scale of one to ten . . ." or "This is a five-star restaurant." Sometimes the adjective itself may help, quite apart from using the comparative or superlative form. Words like *egregious*, or *stupendous*, *infinitesimal*, or *mammoth* can fill the bill. Since any of these words reflect our subjective and relative assessments, we are stuck with the inability to calibrate them. In order to communicate our assessments effectively, given such linguistic imprecision, it pays to avoid hyperbole or emotion-laden words and to try to emulate the scientific mode.

There is more to be said about imprecision in our use of descriptive terms as well as in the way we formulate our opinions, but that will come in a larger context in later chapters. Before them, however, some pesty bits of grammar just can't go unmentioned.

Beware the Negative

Consider how often we say something like, "I don't think that's the case at all." This is perfectly good English, but hardly precise, for it's not a case of our not thinking. What we really mean is, "I think that's not the case at all." It may be nitpicky to take issue with such common phraseology, but the position of the negative in a sentence can be important. As was pointed out earlier, we hear phrases from lawyers and politicians, such as: "There is no evidence of corruption." That's quite different, however, from saying, "There is evidence of no corruption." Saying the former is not meant to obfuscate (one hopes); it's accepted phraseology, but it masks the fact that evidence could have been lost, destroyed, or simply not obtained. In such usage, not all people are that careful, or all people are not that careful.

Only can wander around a sentence and change its meaning. Ooops! An ambiguity slipped in because of the referent "its." I mean the meaning of the sentence, not the meaning of *only*. Think of how the sentence meaning would change if in the statement, "Only my brother went to the movies last night," we placed *only* after *brother, went, the,* or *movies*. It bears emphasis: Precision, precision, precision!

As a final point, the business of the referent can be a sticking point in conveying meaning effectively. Suppose we read, "The senate sent a bill to a subcommittee that authorized research expenditures." Was it the bill or the subcommittee that did the authorization? The correct grammatical interpretation of that sentence would be that it was the subcommittee because the word *that* refers to its immediate antecedent. If the statement had related to the bill, *that* should have been *which* preceded by a comma.

All of the above deals with mechanical details, the nuts and bolts of language, but there is more subtle stuff to deal with. One item has to do with word choice, as it affects accuracy and precision. Take the word *exacerbate*, which might be considered a fancy word. Many people feel that those who use "big" words are pretentious, and those who are familiar with these words may avoid them for the same reason. Writers are often urged to use simple words wherever possible. But these "fancy" words exist for a reason: They represent the fine-tuning of meaning that languages have developed.

Why couldn't one say "worsen," using two syllables instead of the four-syllable word? The answer is that *worsen* is too general; it may be accurate, but not precise. If one used *aggravate*, that would have an unintended connotation, such as when a parent says to a nagging child, "Don't aggravate me!" *Exacerbate* has the connotation of a situation that is being worsened—something in the realm of business or politics, for example.

General semanticists (see next chapter) refer to a more subtle but very powerful aspect of understanding the word(s) you hear or read as "multi-ordinality." That is, even where there is no lexical ambiguity, the significance of the word in its context has to be considered. Think of the word *life* and the value given to the word in the following cases: In the light-hearted, "Life is just a bowl of cherries;" in a person's annoyed response, "Hey, get a life!" to"We are pro-life," in the context of the debate about abortion. Any substantive word ought to be considered in this way.

Dictionaries, which list connotations as well as the more straightforward denotation, are the only standard for the meanings of words. Still, it is difficult to calibrate meanings, for the meaning of words depends on still other words, and so on *ad infinitum*. This is the problem that Wittgenstein tried to resolve.

This regressive dependence on prior references exists even for scientists, whose instruments must be calibrated against accepted standards. Yet even those standards change as knowledge advances. Whereas a yard was once determined by the length of King Canute's arm and the meter eventually established by the length of a platinum bar kept at constant temperature in a Paris vault, length is now measured by the wavelength of light emitted by a beam of argon. So, too, do the connotations and usages of words change. To efficiently communicate one's meaning and to properly evaluate what another person is saying, be it in small arguments or in international diplomacy, one has to be very aware and careful about the choice of words. Shades of Relativity and of Uncertainty!

How to resolve the dilemma between avoiding big words yet being precise on the one hand and insuring understanding on the other? In part, the problem comes about because descriptive words are generalizations. Here, too, science offers an answer. But for this you must read the next chapters.

CHAPTER 3

Generalizations:
People are Always Silly

"Things aren't as good as they used to be." "Everybody's getting divorced these days." "Kids have no respect anymore!" We hear these platitudes continually, summing up the state of the world with quick, pat, definitive judgments. They are no doubt harmless; there is little we feel that we can do about the situations they represent.

Other evaluations are more specific. A husband is told by his wife, "You're never around when I need you!" A parent angrily tells a child, "You never listen to me when I call you!" So it may be with a boss who judges an employee's behavior, and so on up the scale of relationships to when, in the decades of the Cold War, the then Soviet Union was described by the United States as never adhering to international agreements. Such opinions, each on its own scale, can lead to despair or turmoil and can affect what we do about these situations. As evaluations, each is a generalization that may come from different impulses: a verbalized sigh, a dispensing of folk philosophy by which we demonstrate our wisdom to knowing fellow-sufferers, or perhaps utterances to avoid in-depth details when we want to dramatize a point.

Generalizations come out of our mouths in many guises. They may be vague, abstract concepts (e.g., honor, dignity) or stringent extremes (epithets, such as liar, traitor). They may be offered as undelineated, collective words (e.g., the homeless, immigrants) or platitudinous phrases that may be pompous pronouncements ("We must rid ourselves of hatred") or simplistic judgments ("The problem is that . . ." or "The solution is to . . ."). They may be overall opinions or specific stereotypes ("The Jews control the media.") Such statements may be combined, of course, as in, "The homeless are all a bunch of lazy drunkards, and they should be locked up!"

Once enunciated, these generalizations reinforce themselves by a circular process. They become rules of thumb that guide other judgments and steer our behavior. So it is important to understand how they come about and what functions they serve.

The How and Why of Generalizations

Generalizing is a product of perception that starts from the very first sensations an infant responds to. The complex and perplexing things we observe on each occasion gradually strike similar responses to something we have experienced before. As will be seen in the chapter "Perceptions," we extract some of these similarities and gradually sort them into groups. The complexities then become simplified, and the perplexities diminish. Hence, generalizations make it easier for us to understand our perceptions by giving order to the profusion of impressions that bombard us.

As we grow, we fit new observations into the groupings that already exist. Thus we maintain patterns that are familiar and comfortable. By providing a basic fabric that we fill in with the colorful details, generalizing may have aesthetic value. The extent to which we do this depends upon how discerning we are of all the aspects involved and the significance that we give to them.

Similarly, we label these generalizations with words that language already provides. Now the boxes into which we can place new experiences are even more identifiable, and we can share our sense of them with other people by the code words we have given them. This gives generalizations pragmatic value too.

Gradually, we develop faith in the categories we have set up. We think of them as established facts, almost as part of our being, rather than mere simplifications. In addition, each pattern provides a *standard of values* by which we judge new perceptions. When we act in response to these similarities of fact and value, we begin to see similarities in the outcomes too. So generalizations also serve as a basis for predictions.

Reinforced in these ways, much as some insects add dabs of their own secretions to establish their nests, generalizations have survival function.

Unfortunately, these perfectly natural modes of thought can often have less desirable outcomes. This is because generalizing is not an orderly process. It is a grab bag of random observations, impressions, and classifications that reflect our inner psychological needs.

In the extreme, only those ideas agreeable to our cognitive structure or to our frame of reference can be admitted to our house of faith. We become dogmatic, unwilling to accept new ideas, and rigid, unable or unwilling to examine those generalizations we already have. Such attitudes are counterproductive. Our lack of flexibility loses the pragmatic value of adjusting to new information and new situations.

When we apply pragmatism to material things, we classify them. With animal life, this relates to ecology and relationships to humans; with vegetable life, it leads to useful information about drugs and ecology; and with minerals it leads to their potential usefulness as ores or for optical or other properties.

Classifying behavior of individuals and, even more so, of groups is obviously more difficult. There are so many more aspects to consider, and the subjects are most likely in a dynamic state, all interrelating in various ways and degrees. Even more tenuous are generalizations about events and situations.

It is especially important for the intangibles in human affairs that we form our generalizations by as rational a method as possible. So it is worthwhile to look at the way scientific-minded people as a model group their observations compared to the way most people do this.

The differences between the layperson and the scientist are mainly matters of degree, determined by training and habit. In what follows, comparisons will be drawn for each aspect.

Quality of Facts

The Layman's Way: Those facts that go into the hopper of generalization may simply be dramatic or appealing in some way. They may not be relevant to the subject we are forming an opinion about. Facts reported by others, which we include in our opinion, may not be accurate, or they may not be understood clearly or specifically enough. These aspects relate to the validity of the evaluation we are making. By validity, I mean that there has to be a meaningful relationship, a relevance, between the isolated fact and the generalization.

The Scientist's Way: How does a scientist know whether or not a particular fact is a valid input to a generalized statement he may make about some issue? He has to choose his data so that he avoids two kinds of error: the sin of omission—ignoring pertinent factors—and the sin of commission—using data that is not accurate or relevant.

The layman has the same responsibility (remember the Witness Oath discussed in Chapter 2), but the scientist's facts are subject to various rigorous tests for their validity. This depends in part on showing the evidence for his facts, in showing their relevance to other facts, and to overall conclusions by numerical or statistical relationships. Whereas the layman's conclusions if wrong may not have serious effects, the scientist's evaluations may be serious, so he is obligated to devote whatever time (and patience) is needed to develop an iron-clad case.

Hence, the scientist's inputs cannot be gathered by whim. His observations have to be capable of being manipulated as to their presence, absence, and degree. Furthermore, they will be subject to the following logical conditions:

A) The results shall have occurred only when certain facts were put in; the results cannot follow from extraneous inputs (as the sins mentioned above indicate). Conversely, when those inputs are used in repeated tests, they are required to lead to the same outputs with a high degree of statistical probability.

B) A change in the inputs has to result in a corresponding change (in any direction) in the outputs.

C) The regularity or rate of change of the inputs has to produce a corresponding change in the outputs. The rates and direction of change in results need not be the same as those for the inputs, but there needs to be a consistent pattern to the results.

One can see that these conditions are difficult for the layman to track. Fuzzy inputs can lead to incorrect inferences. For example, consider an individual's weight gain. This will increase from childhood at the same time as the population, yet there is no relationship between the two. The only way such increases could be related would be if population increase somehow resulted in higher food production and availability such that the individual could benefit from this. Obviously, one cannot manipulate population in order to demonstrate such a relationship. This seemingly silly example nevertheless illustrates the kind of "pop statistics" that layman latch onto, but the relationship is not valid because it could be countered by bringing in many more appropriate factors regarding body weight. This kind of supposed but unexamined relationship is called a post hoc fallacy, which will be described below.

A more troublesome, ever-present issue is that of relating intelligence to ethnicity. The quality of the factors considered by a scientific outlook ought to depend on defining specifically what we mean by intelligence (see Fig.1), what ethnic facts are involved, what specific relationships are measured, and what kinds of relationships could exist.

Fig. 1.Conceptions of the descriptive term *intelligence.*

a) Fuzzy conception of intelligence. b) Clearer conception of intelligence.

The layperson tends to use these concepts in a vague way, the scientist is required to examine how these aspects are measured and how valid the tests are. The layman tends to be satisfied with his biases, conscious or unconscious, but the scientist has to check to see whether his results, positive or negative, could have been affected by some unconscious bias in the way the variables were chosen, manipulated, and measured. He cannot choose his variables by whim, though intuition may often come into play. The factors investigated have to be built upon previous experiments that need further probing or that suggest new variables to explore.

Also, the variables chosen need to be subject to a pretest to "iron out the bugs." That is, a preliminary experiment needs to be run to ensure that the factors chosen are consistent with the test methods and with the probable results. This regimen establishes the internal validity of the experiment. For instance, testing of people done after lunch may yield different results than if done in the morning when minds are fresh.

Furthermore, the external validity has to be established, that is, the relationship of this artificial test to the real world. Many experiments run by PhD candidates, of necessity, use college students or people in selected institutions like hospitals. The results of these investigations therefore may not have external validity to the general population. Also, Heisenberg's principle of the effect of measuring on the measured is to be borne in mind.

Time is also a factor in external validity. Once a long-term experiment is completed, the conditions that existed at the beginning of the experiment may have changed by the time the results are applied. Facts or their significance may change with time even though we keep to our original observation (as with memories of the "good old days"). Our frame of reference might have changed from when we first observed a thing. These also affect reliability.

Quantity of Facts

Most people get their facts at random. We usually don't consciously seek out information other than what we get from the news media on those matters that we generalize about for social or even political conversation. We tend to read the newspapers or magazines and listen to the radio and TV programs that agree with our viewpoints. Dramatic appeal may lead us to add isolated, infrequent observations to our inventory. These quantitative aspects affect the reliability of our generalizations.

Scientific evaluations, by contrast, need to take a sample size that will produce results that are reliable to a statistical degree. Where possible, the sample size has to reflect the size of the overall population that would be affected by the results of the study. In order to eliminate the chance that certain attributes in a group of people chosen for an investigation may accidentally bias the results, individuals are assigned numbers, but only those numbers listed in a "random numbers table" (a statistical tool) will be chosen for the final tests.

Relationships of Observations

As mentioned above, apparent similarities may lead us to consolidate an evaluation. Our analogies may be imperfect, but we usually don't consciously ask ourselves whether they include the same type of actors, actions, dynamics, and outcomes as the comparable situation.

A legislator, for example, may oppose a bill forbidding discrimination against gays in housing, claiming that this is analogous to letting a harmful germ loose in the community. Equating a gay lifestyle with a germ may have similarities to the legislator, yet one ought to ask if the dynamics of spreading an idea are similar to those of spreading bacteria, whether equating humans to microbes is appropriate, whether the consequences are equivalent, and so on. A more appropriate analogy would involve comparing groups of people, lifestyles, or social problems.

One may also confuse an immediate cause or effect with an underlying long-term cause or effect. A melée between police and young black people may be likened to some incident, such as rowdiness at a rock concert. Such a lumping together of juvenile fracases would be simplistic if the immediate cause of the problem at the musical event, crowding at the entryways, for example, was equated with underlying, long-term causes, such as frustrations over economic conditions and resentment against harsh police attitudes.

In making such generalizations, we show a tendency toward one-way thinking from an apparent cause to an immediate effect. Instead, each cause ought to be seen as an effect of something prior, as part of an ongoing process.

How We Make the Relationships

Whether we're aware of it or not, putting two and two together is the sum of two kinds of mental exercise, each the companion of the other.

Analysis comes first, continually breaking down our impressions into individual facts, relationships, variability of degrees, relevance, and significance of each, with time, and so on. It's like examining a multi-strand piece of rope. Each strand has to be considered separately, examining it for its component threads and those for their individual fibers, even down to the nature of the materials used.

Consider any of the major vexing issues of our time, such as prosecuting a teen-age murderer where capital punishment may be the penalty. Should the person be tried as a juvenile or as an adult? What are the consequences of each? What are the five W's and the one H of the case, for the murderer, the victims, or society? Such situations usually cause us, as individuals and as society, to have a gut reaction, an emotion-driven evaluation.

Yet this breaking down into components is necessary before we can build a useful opinion. Most people do this kind of analysis to some degree unconsciously most of the time. Unfortunately, this half of the process is not apt to be done consciously or systematically because we are not trained to do so as scientists are. It takes time, which the scientist is obliged to spend, and a studious temperament. As a result, we are likely to jump from unwarranted assumptions to foregone conclusions.

Synthesis, or unscrambling our observations, implies that we have to put the parts together again. Enter our frame of reference, our mindset, and our biases. For instance, we abhor crime and regret poverty. We may feel the government should come down hard on the former, yet feel cynical about its ability to control the latter. Yet the two are related on many dimensions, aren't they? Putting together our thoughts about how each is related to education, parenting, and socioeconomic conditions would lead to more temperate judgments and direct us toward more effective solutions. It's easy to agree to such nostrums, but too often our efforts (e.g., votes, volunteer work, etc.) hang on peremptory opinions about the individual aspects in isolation, not on interrelationships.

Again, capital punishment, abortion, and military ventures all involve the taking of human life. If we analyze each issue for that aspect, do we evaluate each one by tying them together for their relationship to this underlying similarity?

Discerning trends is another form of synthesis. In a changing situation, one can fail to see the forest because of a preoccupation with the trees of incidents separated widely in time. Changes in lifestyle, patterns of legislation, or Supreme Court decisions are a few examples of long-term trends that we may fail to take into account, but which may have provided the content for incidents we complain about. Conversely, we often view with alarm events that seem to point to a trend but are really random and unrelated.

A person with a scientific background has a set of protocols for ensuring that the observations that get tied together for an evaluation are valid and relevant. There are mathematical tests, which ordinarily aren't used by the layman. The latter is apt to use a loose tallying of numbers, leading to such egregious clichés as "trouble comes in threes." But the discerning layman can certainly cross-check the consistency and reproducibility of observations, which is part of the scientific protocol.

Despite rigorous procedures, many investigations produce contradictory results, which can drive the reader crazy. One says coffee is good for you, another says it's not. Well, life is complex, and science isn't perfect. What must one do? A further scrutiny of the experiment factors has to be made. Were the coffee-drinkers' lifestyles examined, and if so, for what factors? If similar age groups were checked, at what ages did they start drinking coffee, and so on and so on. Einstein's Relativism and Heisenberg's measurement effects are hovering over the best efforts.

To analyze and synthesize takes time. Impulsiveness and the self-satisfaction of making instant judgments don't allow analysis and synthesis to occur and can lead us to commitments that are hard to change.

Cause and Effect

A grossly misleading type of synthesis that results from inadequate analysis is a fallacy so common that it has a fancy Latin name: Post Hoc Ergo Propter Hoc, which means "After this, therefore because of this." It shows up when people associate two or more events that occur closely in time such that the earlier one is thought to be a cause of the later one. This type of reasoning usually involves some troublesome or dramatic situation.

Although motivated by childish guilt, when a child feels that his parents divorced because he was naughty, he is thinking with this type of fallacious reasoning. A popular advertisement claimed that people in Soviet Georgia who ate a lot of yogurt lived to be one hundred years old. Medical science often runs up against people who are "miraculously" cured "because" they followed some non-medical regimen. Such evaluations are facile and often amount to superstition. To be valid, they would require a lot of statistical evidence factoring in other aspects.

This type of fallacy is very powerful because of the complexities of life where many events may recur over the same time period so as to seem to represent a trend. We may say things like, "All this increase in crime is because of the violence on TV." A potentially more devastating example of this reasoning occurred during the Cold War, when it was said that the policy of deterrence worked because no war had broken out between the US and the then USSR. Undoubtedly this was true, but as a matter of reasoning, there was no way to prove the causal relationship. One could not compare before-and-after periods with all of the same conditions except for the presence or absence of a policy of deterrence.

Therefore, one has to strike a balance between examining *how many* events recur and whether or not they do so *under the same circumstances*. Politicians and advertisers, among others with self-serving interests, try to look "scientific" by showing slyly chosen statistical evidence for such connections. Conversely, authorities will often claim, supported by a selective choice of data, that there is no statistical evidence to show causal connections, as in economic, social, or environmental matters.

Statistics is such an abused discipline as to give rise to the popular saying, "Figures don't lie, but liars do figure." However, the scientific community has sophisticated weapons to evaluate what is appropriate wheat from the rhetorical chaff. These will be discussed in a simplified manner in Chapter 13.

Abstracting

Generalizing has another dimension that is a source of problems: We not only categorize observations, we rank them in hierarchies of type and value. "Higher" generalizations abstract successively fewer of the characteristics held in common by the "lower" groupings. Ignoring differences between the two groupings results in equating the higher levels with more deeply held values. Any substantive word (noun, verb, adjective, or adverb) amounts to an abstraction for the many macro-observations about something that is shared with those of similar referents.

This situation has been aptly illustrated by Alfred Korzybski, the founder of a communication discipline called "general semantics" that deals with the way we form our evaluations. Korzybski developed the "structural differential." I have retained its conception, but have reversed its position (Fig. 2). This schematically shows the increasingly rarified levels of reality that we deal with. Each higher level is a generalization of selectively chosen characteristics from the level beneath it.

Above the verbal level, the abstractions are more conceptual, and this is where the trouble begins. That is because, once we get beyond the functional hierarchy for material things (e.g., fish, animal life, organic matter, product of nature), we can branch off into more intellectual groupings. Those are apt to be more subjective evaluations, so they can be the cause of mutual misunderstandings. This is especially so for intangibles.

For example, one ranking might be abortion, medical procedure, and human activity while another set might be abortion, harmful/beneficial act, sin/free choice. (We need not consider here other hierarchies, such as word, verb, grammatical unit, or concept, mental activity, etc.)

One can see that this process can depend upon one's accessibility to facts, education, naiveté, frame of reference, and mindset. Inaccurate perception or loose judgment might misclassify some lower order under a higher one.

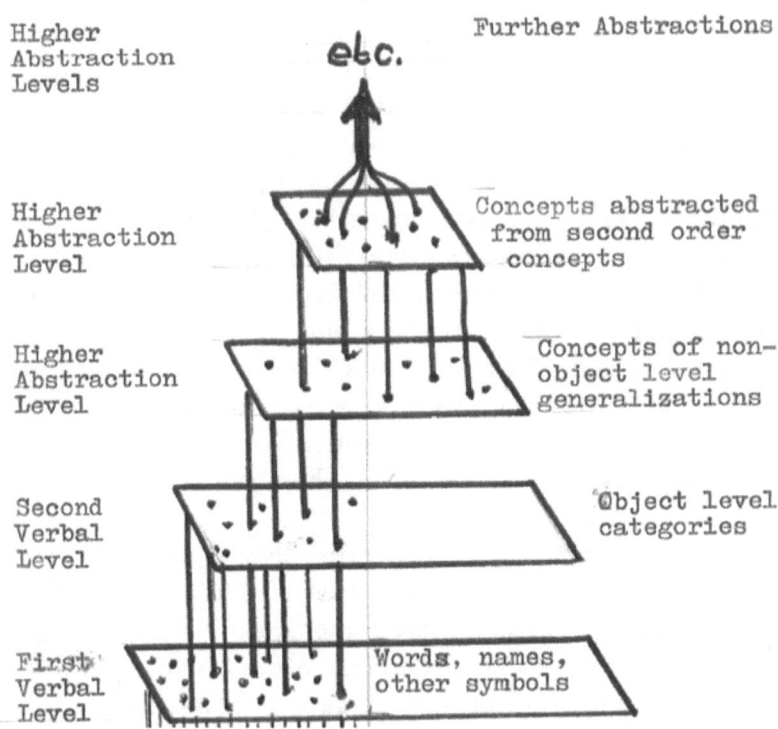

Fig.2. A Structural Differential (Adapted from Alfred Korzybski, *Science and Sanity,* **(Lakeville, CT: International Non-Aristotelian Library Publishing, 1953), p. 393.)**

Calling a whale a fish, for instance, is a matter of incorrect knowledge, but classifying abortion in either a functional hierarchy or a value-related one will be more contentious.

Placing individuals, ideas, or human behaviors into such hierarchies is something we all do. Politicians capitalize on the non-definitive, subjective and emotion—or value-loaded aspects of concepts in their rhetoric. When done by teachers, legal authorities, psychiatrists, and others, misclassifications can be devastating to the people they deal with. Scientists confine themselves to technical hierarchies. Fortunately, they don't get involved with value judgments, except as individual people.

Expression of Opinion

Our impressions, comprehension, and evaluation of things usually exist as general ideas in our minds; we formulate very few of them into words. When we express them, even when requested to do so in formal situations, they are often loosely worded, perhaps somewhat incoherently. Our terms are not defined nor do we check our listener's comprehension by asking that person to repeat to us his or her interpretation of what we said. Each person is apt to assume that the other understands the words as the speaker intended.

If we were to ask each listener in each instance to repeat what was said, we would appear annoyingly didactic, as this is usually done only in cases of specific instructions. We often do ask, "Do you know what I mean?" but it is considered to be a manner of speech, and, at most, may get a nod of the head. Thus, loose generalizations become even looser when expressed and more so when interpreted. Feedback is another issue that will be covered later.

By contrast, scientific expressions are usually so detailed and specific as to be deadly dry and dull. Terminology is defined usually by the function that is represented. And, as described earlier, quantitative data proliferate with great care given to the proper decimal places and tolerances.

When an ordinary person says, "I have a theory that . . . ," he is actually stating a hypothesis. This is what the scientist formally starts with—not a simple guess or preference, but a rational likelihood that uses evidence. The experiment will warrant replication or fine-tuning by many other such trials. Only after repeated demonstrations to the satisfaction of a professional scientific organization will the conclusions be honored with the status of "theory."

There is a hook in this, however. *Proof* involves another difference between the layman's and the scientist's claims. Some outstanding relationship may be considered as proof by the layman,. *Conclusions* are expressed with different degrees of assuredness between the layman and the scientist. The former is too often not willing to accept doubt about his opinions. The scientist, though, knows that it is impossible to prove that something doesn't exist, for sometime, somewhere, that thing may show up. Proof for the existence or nonexistence of something requires evidence. So, with characteristic caution, the scientist pursues his quest with a hypothesis that is the *opposite* of what he wants to demonstrate, and then goes about *disproving* his claim with evidence. The results, however, are never considered absolute proof, even when they rise to the status of theory, for even they may be overthrown in time as more evidence is accumulated.

Summary

Generalizations are a normal way for people to make sense of observations by giving structure to all our impressions to form evaluations. As made by the ordinary person, the observations may be limited in number, randomly gathered or retained, and are possibly transitory. Their relationships are apt to be based on loosely assumed similarities or subjective analogies, not systematically analyzed for their pertinence or significance. As evaluations, they may be impulsively formed and grouped into categories that are dimly perceived and ranked. Validity, reliability, and responsibility to challenge are often of a low order. When expressed, these generalizations may sound like certainties, but are apt to be loosely phrased, and feedback for the way they are understood is very often not sought or offered.

Rigor and attitude are the two aspects that differentiate scientists from the average person in the way they generalize. The high degree of rigor that we associate with the way a scientist discusses a subject applies to continually analyzing ever-finer components, methodically seeking relationships at each step, and testing conclusions for validity and reliability. To be methodical requires dedication to ferret out an indisputable answer, and this requires patience and perseverance. Additionally, the scientist needs humility, for he or she knows that conclusions are continually challenged and must show their worth by leading to sound predictions.

This is not to say that the average person doesn't make assessments so that he can use them for future situations. Many people do form their opinions in the spirit of scientific thinking, even if they do not do so with the purposefulness, rigor, or persistence of the scientist.

One may protest, "Who can go through all of these details and shenanigans considering the realities of daily life?" The point is that the rigor of the scientists' mode is a model and reminder for more effective evaluating.

CHAPTER 4

Stereotypes: The Metal Plate-In Our Heads

The previous chapter was a generalization about generalizations. A specific yet common type of generalization is the stereotype, which originally referred to a plate made of metal or other rigid material that could be used to widely replicate written or pictorial material. The connotation most commonly used today refers to the sameness thought to be shared by a group of people or events. The impression, therefore, is the one in our heads, and as evaluations, they can be troublesome.

Stereotypes are usually applied to people as to their political, social, religious, or cultural attributes, but they can also be applied to situations. Stereotypes are usually inaccurate because they consist of selectively chosen characteristics. As such, they are simplifications that reflect our biases. Historically, they have been perpetuated by ignorance and social pressures, doing great harm to individuals and groups. But they can also lead to facile judgments about situations that prevent effective assessments, so one is obliged to expect that these aren't modes of categorizing that scientists would adopt. Stereotypes may show up as a general statement, a descriptive term, or a label or they may simply exist in a person's head as an opinion. When we say a person is intelligent, for example, there might be little quarrel if someone disagreed. If we ascribe that person's intelligence to a whole group of people who are similar in some respects, we are in deeper waters. What exactly do we mean by "intelligent" and how discretely can we apply this to other members of the group? Are all politicians crooked, are all lawyers out for the money, are all members of some national group stupid? When pressed on this, we'll admit, "Of course not!" but the impression lingers and tends to pop up. We think of these characterizations as abstractions in the murky cloud of Figure 1a without bothering to delineate the components of Figure 1b. Referring to the Structural Differential in Figure 2, which details have we left out?

Some terms have more specific connotations that tend to become labels as well as adjectives, e.g., liberal, conservative, etc., which imply that a person is that entire stripe. But a person might be conservative on some issues, liberal on others, or strongly conservative on some issues and less so on others.

In the Iran-Contra issue of the late-Reagan era, there was a purported "Israeli" connection. In an earlier drug-related case, there was a reported "French" connection. Did these refer to the governments, to certain citizens, or to someone born or living there? Similarly, we speak of someone being "a good Christian," when we may be referring to Judaeo-Christian values rather than to the person's actual religion.

Later on, I will talk about, as the general semanticists say, "The word is not the thing; the map is not the territory." The fact that each of us has our own map implies that the direction the word takes you may not be the same as where it takes me. Yet so often, we tacitly accept such descriptive terms, assuming that we are driving with the same map.

These terms are quick, comprehensive, and convenient to use. Does that make them invalid? Must we go into long-winded locutions when we can assume everyone uses the same shorthand?

The problem comes in making that assumption. Apart from breaking down a term or label into its components or the degree of its validity, we need to ask in what specific matters a person can be given such a label. Are we denying ourselves a proper basis for action due to judgments about a person or situation based on facts that are missing and misapprehensions that are added? Does the person always act accordingly and always to the same degree? Does A in the group act the same all the time or to the same degree as B in the same group?

Here is where the concept of a stereotype is most dangerous. We absorb these fuzzy images from what we read and hear from others. We may adopt them because we identify with others who use them. In doing so, we have jumped from the "object level" to the "verbal level" without much scrutiny of the former.

Such untidy generalizations defy the witnesses' oath for assuring sufficiency of observations, avoiding extraneous information, and stating what the witness believes to be the truth. Too few attributes are garnered and may not be factual, and others are ascribed that have no relevance.

In the social arena, stereotyping of minority school children as to their probable intellectual capacities and motivations is known to have placed three strikes against them. Teachers may have lowered expectations for these students when they automatically pre-judge them before actually observing them. Because of the momentum that a stereotype has developed, teachers may devote less attention to these pupils. The children's self-esteem can suffer further, and failure becomes a self-fulfilling prophecy. In turn, this helps to perpetuate the stereotype.

Furthermore, stereotypes aren't objective because they usually have an emotional or psychological component. Using them allows a person to feel superior to the target, especially when one adopts the stereotypes of an in-group. The sense of belonging reinforces the use of this kind of labeling. The certainty with which people hold onto these uninformed opinions provides a shield against the sense of insecurity from the unknown others. In turn, this fear leads to an exaggeration of the selected features of the labeled person or group. Suppressing specific characteristics makes it easier to lump together people in the out-group, which makes them seem larger than life and further reinforcing the stereotype.

So, a stereotype is even stronger than a mere generalization because it can give comfort to the person who likes to have simple, clear, familiar pictures to identify with. Stereotypes, therefore, lend themselves to use by demagogues. Far from being a practical identification, it becomes a weapon for destructive action. It is not simply hanging around as a casual thing for people to latch onto. Too often, it descends to a primitive level as a knee-jerk response to something dramatic. At that level, it becomes the response of the infant as yet unable to discriminate appearance from substance, who calls any man "Dada" or any small animal "doggie." Similarly, a very young child, asked to respond when hearing "cow," will answer "pow." Only as the child matures, will he or she respond to the idea of "bull."

Finally, use of a stereotype is lazy. It takes mental processing time to absorb, sort out, and think about the many aspects of a thing. Many people do not accept the impingement of new information easily nor can they be bothered looking for subtleties.

To the extent that people indulge in this kind of thinking, they are responding with what Korzybski called a "thalamic reaction." He was referring to that primitive part of the brain that is considered to be the seat of our emotions and impulsive reactions. It obviously won't go away, and it does kick in. But the thalamus can be trumped by the convoluted outer portion of the brain, the cortex—which developed later in humankind as it does in individuals—and is the seat of our more mature intellect and reasoning, which should see through stereotypes.

Sadly, even educated, presumably intelligent people can maintain stereotypical views out of prejudice or lack of familiarity with a group of people or a situation.

Isn't a Stereotype Merely Typical?

How can we tell if our views adhere to a stereotype or if they are objectively typical? The answer depends upon the kind and amount of experience we've had with the labeled group, directly or indirectly. It depends, too, on how observant we've been, how willing we are to look for individual differences compared to the whole, and our honesty about our own selectivity. Our empathy toward the target and our tolerance for accepting subtle facts also play a part.

If a person has had many business dealings with people in some Middle Eastern country, contact with any other merchant in that area who is indulging his cultural custom of bargaining, would probably be an example of a typical Middle Easterner. If one meets a person whose name and features evoke that part of the world, but if the encounter is on one's own turf, expecting the other person to indulge in extensive bargaining during a business deal probably would be to engage in a stereotype. In the former situation, one can expect behavior similar to the many others observed; in the latter case, mere name and appearance are not enough to prejudge the individual. So one's attitude and empathy toward another person comes into play.

It is hard to draw the line for many people, as they feel that the stereotype would not exist were it not for an "earned reputation" on the part of the target. Although many of the characteristics of the stereotype may exist in the targeted group, it is the selective choice or exaggeration of these features to the exclusion of other significant characteristics that makes the "earned reputation theory" invalid.

Too often, the stereotype is applied to a group that is strange or disliked in some way. If one shares this reaction, it is at least fair and more efficient to ask what might be the causes for the disliked characteristics.

Understanding cultural habits or economic pressures, for example, would do much to allay the negative image.

Classifying: the Scientific Way

It is the task of the scientist to delineate the features that are typical, to apply a label to any collection that has many features in common. Doing so in a systematic way goes at least as far back as Aristotle, who was a prodigious classifier of everything he came into contact with. This was typical of the ancient Greeks' fascination with the apparent order in the universe. Objects and situations that existed in nature were the givens. They had names, and were the fixed starting points for further study. This led to a deductive approach in seeking explanations. It was as if "Pigs are called pigs because they're so dirty." Great as he was, though, Aristotle left a legacy of deductive thinking that has caused great harm—an issue that will be discussed further in Chapter 10.

Certainly an inductive approach must have been used by early humans when they gave names for many things they observed to be similar. But it was not until the nineteenth century that the intellectual style of making objective observations, independent of any *a priori* categories, really took hold as the mode of science. This style had antecedents going back to the fourteenth century in religious matters and was given its first explicit push in the early seventeenth century by Francis Bacon.

In the 1800s, there was a virtual taxonomic ferment. Plants and animal life were categorized into hierarchies of species, genus, family, and so on up to kingdom. Minerals were similarly classified.

Much of this depended upon physical and chemical analysis. Finding, sorting, and arranging evidence to construct named categories—the inductive method—is the key to the scientist's assurance that he can objectively describe what is typical. By contrast, the old-fashioned approach of assuming that a named object ought to have certain characteristics—the deductive approach—bore the danger of setting up a stereotype. As more observations were made, some didn't fit within the newly established hierarchies. So, back to the drawing board! Sub-categories were set up or items were switched around. The process continues. This fine-tuning also avoids stereotyping.

More significantly, the characteristics observed in something were noted for the *function* they served in relation to others in the same group.

By doing so, grouping may be done for convenience. For example, herbs, which would normally be classified as various groups of flora, could be grouped under generalizations of their medicinal value.

However, this functional grouping can lead to contention, for it isn't names that count, but rather what the named group does that is important. Stereotyping an ethnic group, for example, prevents people from seeing the contributions that individuals within that group can make.

This becomes especially egregious with the supposed category of race. In holding that concept, we overlook the intermingling of people that has gone on for countless millennia. Accordingly, we too often tend to assume that a person of a particular race is wholly, purely of that group. Anthropologists, however, now view race in a functional way, considering it to be any group of people that intermarry (or interbreed) in large numbers. Thus, jetsetters might constitute a "race," as might white collar professionals, farmers, and so on.

Scientists know that nature does not provide these neat categories. Not only is a whale not a fish nor a bat a bird, but substances like viruses bridge the world of the living and the non-living, and bacteria are neither flora nor fauna. Nor are humans totally exempt from ambivalent characteristics, as a significant, if unpublicized, number of hermaphrodites are born.

It is easy to forget that it is we humans, in our normal drive to make sense of the myriad things around us, who put nature into orderly little boxes. Actually, the idea that we live in an orderly universe is akin to a stereotype, resulting from considering only the most obvious, dramatic observations about nature that stand out from the infinitude of unordered and disorganized events around us.

Scientists realize that there is probably a statistical chance that, amongst all the events in the universe, some things will occur in an orderly manner. But even though nature achieves an apparent balance because of action and reaction over long stretches of time, it is mostly chaotic.

In contrast to the non-scientific person who may impute reported or supposed characteristics to a stereotype in a deductive manner, the scientific person will apply names only suitable to evidence, obtained by inductive observation first. Of course, the named categories must be emotion-less, value-less, and objective. Only after these are firmly established as a base can the scientist make deductive inferences of probable outcomes. All of this requires a dispassionate, patient, deliberative attitude.

When people say something like "He's a typical politician," or "When dealing with Jews, you have to . . . ," they are frequently dealing with the stereotypical, not the typical. We need to apply the journalist's five W's and one H to our stereotyped images in order to turn them into pictures that are useful in an efficient way. That is, we must remember to ask who are the actual people involved, who is doing what to whom, what are their characteristics (by observation), when and where do they apply, how are all the elements related, and so on.

Stereotypic labels are not defined clearly, for they depend on the perceptions of the people using them. By contrast, scientific labels are precisely defined by professional organizations. As knowledge gets more refined and connotations change for words used for scientific purposes, the definitions are likewise refined. The definitions are not based loosely on appearances but on their function or something measurable. In keeping with this precision, such terms must be discrete, not overlapping with others that refer to slightly different characteristics.

If the thinking habits ascribed to scientists seem to be merely those of any intelligent person, I would agree, for that is in keeping with my thesis that the scientific mindset is the contemporary paragon for intelligence.

Summary

A stereotype is an inadequate generalization. More than a label, it is an image that selects and exaggerates certain characteristics of a person, group of people, or situation. Although seemingly comprehensive and convenient, it is a quick, essentially lazy, and childlike judgment. As such, it differs from what is numerically typical.

Stereotypes are based partly on lack of information, but they also involve bias. This is often acquired unthinkingly from one's associates or from the media. As such, they have an emotional content that conveys a sense of superiority, comfort, and security against an unfamiliar target. The stereotyped person or group may seem larger than life because of the concentration on the few attributes, which become dramatic. So the stereotype can take on the quality of a magic talisman. The scientist's application of labels, by contrast, goes to well-studied items. They are given precise definitions and are usually related to measurable parameters and functions that are observed or can be inferred with validity. The scientist's use of a term is not value-loaded but refers to objectively observed characteristics.

This approach allows one to refer to what is "typical." Thus, knowledge of the group can yield a valid expectation of the individual member by deduction. Conversely, observation of an individual known to be a member of a group can lead inductively to valid expectations about the group.

So what is the lesson? Ask yourself if the view you hold is really warranted by the facts, and shun stereotypes like the plague!

CHAPTER 5

Polarities:
When Black or White Means Seeing Red

"Tell me, am I right or wrong?" and "Yer either fer us or agin us." How many times have we said or heard those phrases. These either/or evaluations point to our failure to strike a balance between a generalization, often a stereotype, and more in-depth specifics. The danger goes beyond leaving out a quantity of details; it is a matter of the quality of what is left out. Qualifying conditions and subsidiary facts that would help us to form smarter views of the primary facts are omitted. Instead, the one-sided, extreme position comes to represent the whole situation.

This oversimplification or overgeneralization is referred to by general semanticists as "allness." Is there a difference between an either/or statement and a good-or-bad characterization?

Yes, there is, for there are implications for the way scientists size up the world. Regardless of those differences, polarized views can become more dangerous in the common conflicts between groups as large as nations. In "ours" versus "theirs," "ours" is invariably the good and right one, "theirs" the bad and wrong one. It's like a Nazi concentration camp gauleiter directing incoming inmates "to the right or to the left." No third possibility is available.

This style of thinking doesn't depend on the subject matter or its importance. It can relate to passive value-judgments, to beliefs, to opinions, or to actions to be taken. Because they leave no room for variation, extremist views have no tolerance for moderate methods. The timing of putting them into effect may be impulsive, leading to aggressiveness or violence.

When polarized charges are hurled at us, we are stung to the quick and become blinded to the shadings. Objectivity goes out the window. Only the essentials (as we see them) stand out, and we invest these with the burden of what the whole issue means to us. We tend to instinctive, primitive "fight-or-flight" reactions, instead of maturely seeking in-between alternatives. Psychology is doing the talking, not intelligence.

In short, those who size up the world in terms of black-and-white see red as they face one another.

The summary solutions to problems we read about in the media often involve punishment or retribution. The killing of a police officer may lead us to think that capital punishment is too good for the murderer. Our reaction to a tyrant on the world scene (e.g., Ayatollah or Saddam Hussein) is apt to be "Why doesn't someone knock that guy off, drop a bomb on him or something?" At worst, if a populace is uninformed or misinformed and is largely unquestioning, news presented as dramatic oversimplifications bring abstract beliefs of right and wrong, patriotism, and so on into play. Before one can stop it, society has been polarized into an atmosphere that leads to rebellion or war.

What leads us into these evaluative dead-ends? Many reasons: habits of making snap judgments in the heat of the moment, and being opinionated and self-impressed are the more superficial explanations. People may see themselves as so seriously affected by events that they take extreme positions. This would be a substantive basis, but might not be enough to justify the polarized response.

Some people are less analytical than others and can't see the subtler issues or grasp their significance. It is troublesome to have to bother with all the ifs, ands, and buts; it is easier to see things as black or white and not have to bother with the grays. We feel secure with the viewpoint that is most comfortable for us or with the one that is easiest to grasp. One is compelled, therefore, to accept all of one position and none of the other. Decision-making becomes easier—you take it or leave it. This is a partial answer on an intellectual plane.

An emotional component may enter. Uncertainty, insecurity, and frustration lead many of us to grasp for the easiest, most comprehensive, seemingly most available answer to the problem or perplexity. Hence we take refuge in it and cling to it.

Further, the substantive issues may involve deeply held beliefs that conditioning makes us incapable of giving up; indeed, we feel threatened if these beliefs are challenged. The opposing viewpoint may threaten our very security and evoke fear beyond any more pragmatic problems. When the strength of our beliefs or our psychological investment in the values of some subject is high, and when two positions on the subject are seen as contradictions of each other, we tend to dig in our heels about the view we favor. There appears to be no third way, as each position represents all of the good or all of the bad points.

It's great and satisfying to be able to expiate this fear by striking back at whatever or whoever deeply troubles us and to do so definitively. The Good Guy/Bad Guy scenarios of popular entertainment do that for us. These fictional prototypes have a lingering appeal to the child that remains within each of us. Heroes and villains of folklore have the clarity that children need; only in this simplistic fashion can they grasp the way the world works. Unfortunately, such childlike assessments carried into adulthood are applied by many of us in important matters. This is the psychology that politicians appeal to.

Soviet Premier Krushchev's saying that he will bury the US, President Reagan's characterization of the Soviets as "The Evil Empire," and George W. Bush's "Dead or Alive" search for terrorists are prominent demonstrations of these childlike assessments. Lifting such a polarized view out of our folklore appeals to the populace who want quick, simple, assertive images to latch onto.

Aren't some polarized positions warranted though? What about a businessman, judge, or parent who says, "I want a yes or no answer. Don't give me any 'maybes.'" In many cases, no in-between position is possible. In such cases, the "ifs" and "maybes" should have been discussed beforehand, providing a fall-back position for contingencies. The process of reaching a decision is analogous to what happens in a computer.

These devices involve sequences of electronic switches. As with an ordinary electric switch, its operations are contradictory—it is either on or off (unless it chatters). Each switch, however, triggers another switch and so on in a cascade (represented by the binary numbering system of ones and zeros). This is in effect the way life works in most cases; it is analogous to a summation of various routes through all the micro on-off transistors that make up the chips in the computer. It is also the normal process by which people make wise decisions, consciously or not. Too frequently, though, peremptory, unwise decisions are made because issues are viewed solely in terms of contradictory alternatives. This obviously doesn't provide room in one's thinking for the various interacting inputs or outputs of a situation.

It's all very well to understand the bases for polarized thinking in others, but do we see this in ourselves? On a cognitive level are dogmatic mindsets, an aspect that will be dealt with in later chapters.

As to the two types of polarities referred to earlier—either/or or good/ bad—the former is a *contradictory* statement, all or nothing. One can't be "a little bit pregnant." The latter is a *contrary* one. It covers "allness" over a whole range of possibilities, for a person or situation can be somewhere in between, or good in some respects while bad in others at the same time.

Contradictories

Contradictory words are mutually exclusive. An object may be made entirely of wood or not; a student may pass a course or fail. In this sense, a contradictory can be a negation, bringing to mind Aristotle's Law of Contradiction and his Law of the Excluded Middle—another topic to tantalize you with, but which will be covered in Chapter 10.

The belief in duality harkens back to Plato, who, trying to explain change and variability of things, held that the essence of reality was not in what met the eye but was in a class of abstractions, or the Ideals. Aristotle's attempt to clarify an explanation of what things were by laying out principles of A and Non-A lingered through the ages. This thinking fit very nicely into the body/soul, transient/eternal, material/spiritual, evil/ good, Devil/God concepts of the religions of succeeding centuries.

The tacit assumption of irreconcilable opposites exists in more subtle, less dramatic forms than those of political or religion dogmatism. We still retain a sense of duality in many social issues. It is easy for us to think of the criminal as being a "bad seed," having "bad blood," or as having come from a bad family. Yet so often when a crime is committed by someone who people know, their neighbors will say in a television interview, "He was so quiet, such a gentleman always. His people are nice, middle-class folks." It is as though there can be no coexistent mix of good and bad for highly specific characteristics. What seems to be a contradictory characterization in these instances should be thought of as a contrary one. There are more examples.

In our times, the psychological ambivalence of gender has been publicized. This has made us aware of the possible lack of a sharp and absolute distinction between male and female, at least as far as such subtle aspects as hormonal variations go. For example, a significant number of hermaphrodites are born each year, but are quietly corrected surgically. In medicine, our awareness of psychosomatic illness indicates that the mind and body are not two separate states that exist as polar opposites. Yet this apparently still must be learned by many doctors, who we hear must learn to take the patient's emotional health in mind in their bedside manner.

Throughout this discussion, I have been using a typographic device that attempts to accommodate these dichotomies on the mundane level of daily communication. This is done by using a slash mark (or hyphen) to show in writing what would be a quick liaison in speech for seemingly opposed but intrinsically related terms like "space/time," "Judeo/Christian," and so on. With no convenient term in English to bridge the genders, as mentioned earlier, "he/she" (and similar forms) has become a way to avoid the careless monopoly of the male pronoun. These devices let us express a valid "allness" to unite the polar extremes of contradictories.

Contraries

In hurried conversations, pretty/ugly and good/bad may seem to be contradictory, but they are merely opposites in a continuum of many increments. Here again, objectivity and specificity come into play, for such evaluations are highly subjective.

When Shakespeare's Hamlet Polonius advises, "Neither a borrower nor a lender be," he was really engaging in a contrary statement, however wise, for one can borrow and lend on occasion and in judicious amounts and without harm in most cases. However, when Patrick Henry said, "Give me liberty, or give me death!" he was engaging in an all-or-nothing type of choice that was, linguistically at least, unbalanced. Death is absolute, but what constitutes liberty, and how much of it is involved in the all-of-it that his statement implies?

The average reader may absolve himself of this habit. Knowing his own mind, he may feel that any statement that comes out of his mouth is a simple, clear evaluation based on many aspects adequately contemplated. One hopes that is the case. For many of us, however, an unequivocal judgment may not have been so fully prepared. Think how readily we may blurt out in an argument, "You're a liar," "He's stupid," or "She's brilliant." The fact that these are extremes of their class does not mean that they may not be valid. The problems arise when they are not warranted. A more temperate term, less driven by emotion, may be more objective.

Avoiding the term and giving a behavioral example would be even more appropriate and effective.

To some extent, this may depend upon one's vocabulary, though most people can find appropriate words or phrases to express intermediate positions. But the language, even though provocative, is only superficially the problem; it is the underlying evaluation that is polarized.

Though judgmental terms primarily concern qualities, they may be quantitative, too, and this lends them to some sort of measurement. Poll-takers and linguistics approach an assessment of opinions and attitudes by using variations of the Semantic Differential (Fig. 3). Developed originally by Charles Osgood, it involves a matrix of two columns of words with seven columns of spaces in between. The left and right columns have words that are contraries—one extreme listed at the end of each line. The spaces in between are used to place a checkmark for the user's evaluation of the degree to which that line characterizes the subject of the poll or whatever is being evaluated. Osgood categorized the word pairs into groups that he felt could be drawn from many cultures. These groups are activity, potency, and evaluation.

As the words imply, activity has to do with anything in motion, potency with the degree to which a characteristic exists, and evaluation with emotions or perceptions. However, the distinctions are not clearly drawn. One might consider that "hot/cold," "sharp/dull," and "angular/rounded" are words of quality that express degree and so might be considered as potency words, whereas they are considered to be activity words.

People of normal sensitivity and average education undoubtedly evaluate things with their own unconscious equivalent of a semantic differential, however loosely. One could critique the use of this tool for its applicability. For example, how much value would one place in forming an opinion about someone between a liar/truth-teller characteristic and a suspicious/trusting characteristic? This only illustrates the complexity of the nuance of contrary terms. There's no need to go into that here, but a more formal use of this tool in English classes could provide a model to get us into the habit of calibrating the descriptive words we use, read, or hear.

Fig. 3 THE SEMANTIC DIFFERENTIAL

To analyze the connotative meaning of any concept, e. g , Government Welfare, place an X in one of seven positions on each horizontal scale. "Good" and "Bad" in this Figure represent polar opposites only for part of the Evaluative scale. Other words listed vertically in the far left and far right columns represent the Activity and Potency scales.[3]

VARIOUS Good_____,. _____, _____, _____. _____ _____, _____Bad POLAR
WORDS*   ex-   quite   fairly neutral fairly quite   ex-   OPPOSITES*
            T remely good   good   bad   bad   tremely
               Good   bad

*Words in the vertical columns represent dimensions of activity, potency and evaluation; but those conforming to these categories are scrambled, and the polar opposites are scrambled from left to right. This is to avoid a "set" where responses would be influenced by one another.

Application to Time

The idea behind the Semantic Differential also applies to the way we express time. Our evaluations of time factors as they relate to events or people's behaviors—how often things happen, how long they last, how long the intervals are between events, and the regularity of these occurrences—are often too broad. We typically think in terms of "always" and "never."

The complaints of the spouse and the parent given at the beginning of Chapter 3 on generalizations typify this. In business, too, it is not uncommon to hear a remark like, "How come our competitor always gets there first?" or "How come we never had these problems before?" Our orientation toward polarized thinking anesthetizes us, especially in

---

[3]   Words are scrambled vertically within each category, and the polar opposites are scrambled horizontally. This is to avoid a "set" where responses would influence one another.

situations of stress, to the less memorable cases that occurred in between. Hence the good rule: Always remember to never say "always" and "never."

Of course, there are situations for which we can validly use these terms. One can never know all the facts about everything that ever existed; one can never walk unaided into space. We can assume that the sun will always rise, and that humans, unlike Methuselah, will never live to be nine hundred years old. Yet, as a state of imaginative open-mindedness, however much in the realm of scientific fantasy, we can at least speculate that the sun's rise could change if some giant asteroid with a cycle of millions of years were to hit the earth, as some scientists feel may have happened in the past. Similarly, if humans can be frozen in suspended animation for extended space travel, the life span of that biblical old man might become possible. Indeed, we can assume that time will continue and that there will always be an "always."

"Always" and "never" are used as shorthand. The problems with them arise when we substitute them for events that do or do not appear in daily life. Too frequently, the word becomes the thing, and the mindset of polarity becomes our reality. We should really be saying and thinking "virtually always" or—with Captain Corcoran in Gilbert and Sullivan's *Pinafore*—"hardly ever."

The Mode of Science

This tentative attitude is more nearly that of science. "Always" can be ambiguous, meaning "for all time" or "on all occasions." As to the latter, a scientist would factor such a description more discretely, drawing a distinction between "continuously" and "continually." The latter, too, would then have to be further described in terms of duration of events, intermittent lapses, and the regularity of each.

As to the meaning of "for all time" as an absolute, the correct model from science that needs to be kept in mind is the asymptote—the axes of X-Y coordinates that are approached closer and closer by a hyperbola but can never be contacted (Fig. 4)

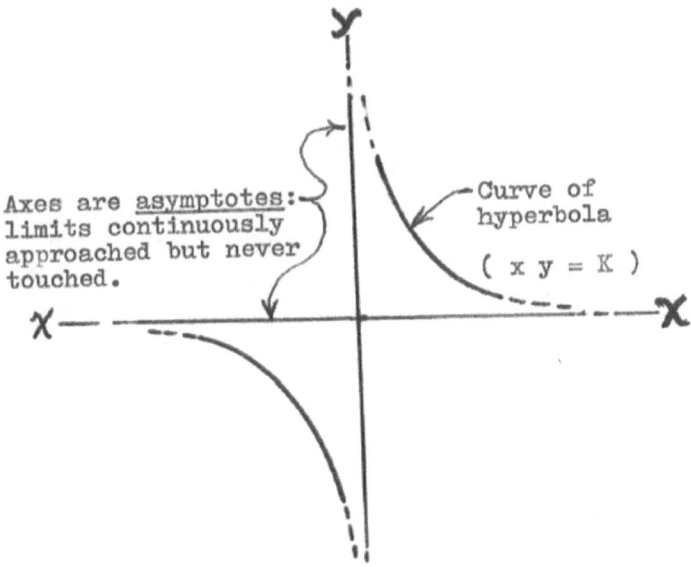

Fig.4. Hyperbolae, showing limits (asymptotes) never reached.

This is similar to the brain teaser that if a frog were to jump from the end of a log to the middle of the log, and then were to keep jumping half of the remaining distance in each leap, it would theoretically never fall off the log.

A Bit of Philosophy

Considering time factors brings science into the realm of philosophy, for science holds the view that there is never an end point. Nor is there ever perfection, which is only an ideal that we must keep striving for. A segment of Jewish thought holds that this could well have been part of the thinking of their ancient predecessors when Jesus was proclaimed the Messiah. For if, in fact, the Messiah came, what would there be to hope for? Even when a specific wish is gratified, we strive for still further rewards. As Alexander Pope said, "Hope springs eternal in the human breast."

It is part of our humanity to maintain the process of seeking what we call positive and good, for those things reflect the essence of the life-thrust. In like manner, scientists know that we will never achieve all the answers, as there will always be more knowledge to gain. The end product is not as important to the scientific view as the process. So there must always be room for skepticism. Unfortunately, this is not the mindset of people who, by smugness or ignorance, feel they have all the answers in a particular case. Nor is it the mindset of people who adopt extreme positions.

We know that constant flux is the predominant state of nature, be it on the subatomic, human, or astrophysical scale, even though we don't discern it equally on all of these dimensions or think about it all the time. While every instant of life can be considered an event, those that we normally bother to evaluate are relatively few compared to the ever-present processes around them. Nor do they occur spontaneously; they have their antecedents, however unperceived. Because events and characteristics in nature and in society exist on a continuum, we need to caution ourselves to express them with contrary rather than contradictory words. Admittedly, the number of spaces between polar terms on a Semantic Differential should be infinite, as should be the gradations in intensity for a given characterization. Realistically, we can mark off only the perceptible differences by the words we have available.

Of course, in nature there are contradictory states: solids, liquids, gases, escape velocities from Earth, fertilization, and conception. Yet even these are viewed by science as limiting events in an ongoing process. A straight line is a limiting condition of a curve, a circle is the limit of an infinite number of infinitesimal straight sides in a polygon, and "rest" is infinitely reduced motion. Changes of state and returns to Earth from space are at least reversible. Rupture of materials can be thought of in larger terms of fabrication and recycling, just as conception of life is part of the larger cycle of death and rebirth.

No one needs a scientific outlook, of course, to know that change is a constant factor of life. But we often act and take positions as if this is not the case. If the scientific mindset were the norm, we would undoubtedly integrate a sense of process into our attitudes and evaluations.

Consider some examples of our ambivalence. For most material things, like labor-saving devices, easier forms of travel, more exciting forms of entertainment, and so on, even as we are pleased to have them, we moan about them when they involve physical encroachments on our environment or increases the pace of life. "Oh, well, that's progress," we sigh. We accept with reluctance the loss of "the good ole days," "the dear, dead days beyond recall," and bemoan, "You can't go home again," as Tom Wolfe titled his novel.

The social, cultural, or economic matters, and more importantly, our beliefs and attitudes, have great inertia. We are not attuned to considering new ideas and attitudes as part of an evolutionary process. Abstractions like freedom, democracy, morality, or lesser intangibles like respectfulness or family values become icons that evoke automatic reverence, even as we participate unwittingly in their transition. It is often hard to see that some behaviors that we considered aberrations became more frequent, were adopted by an *avant garde* (e.g., Bohemians, hippies) and became trendy, developed into a movement, and before we knew it, became a permanent part of our culture. In the meantime, we've remained stuck with older conceptions or generalities of what a labeled idea meant.

This is particularly so with any development that touches moral values, such as birth control, abortion, fetal tissue research, or various biogenetic developments. We prefer to think of morality as a definitive concept, fixed for all time. As an abstraction, it may be so, but the interpretation of what is considered moral may change with time. We cannot accept that "process" implies that the conditions that led to our characterizing a situation in a certain way at a particular time may in fact have changed by imperceptible increments.

Typically, on such issues, we think of the new in comparison with the old; the old, we're sure, was better. We have yet to train our minds so that instinctively we examine the new as part of necessary progress. General semanticists propose a device, whether printed or merely kept in mind, to remind us of this, using subscripts. Thus, situation $_{1a}$ is not the same as situation $_{1b}$. In terms of time, situation$_{1991}$ is not the same as situation$_{1992}$.

Certainly, the progress may not have been for the better. The point of this discussion is that it is counterproductive to decry it automatically because of a fixed view anchored to the past.

Polarity among Scientists

The tendency toward polarized thinking is so ingrained in our habits and in our emotional investment with some ideas that, ironically, even all-too-human scientists are not immune to it. This only shows how big a problem it is to overcome.

Proponents of a favored theory frequently take an either/or stand instead of a more cooperative search for coordination. Intellectual battles have waged for centuries over perception versus reality, over the effect of mind versus body, of heredity versus environment, the wave versus particle theory of light, of the Big Bang versus the Steady-State theories of the universes, to name a few. Experiments can only be concerned with a limited number of factors. The investigator's frame of reference (as will be seen in Chapter 7) is the impediment here. Faith and pride in one's work, not to mention professional and commercial benefits and ego, also cause even professional people to dig in their heels.

Frequently the news media will report on social or economic problems for which various interest groups will suggest the causes or propose solutions. Very often, both are proffered on an either/or basis. To some extent, a both/and approach has been tried in some ventures. This represents progress in the style of thinking, though it depends upon political will and available funds. Demonstration projects for various teaching methods in public schools, methods of farming, use of agricultural chemicals, and various medical regimens are a few examples.

Summary

Expressing situations as either/or positions is a communication style that reflects an oversimplification by the user and can cause an emotional reaction in the listener or reader. Taking extreme, polarized positions can severely limit arriving at wise decisions or effective solutions. One has to be aware of alternatives that are mutually exclusive (contradictories) as opposed to those that exist on a continuum (contraries). With the latter, some of both characterizations can coexist to one degree or another. "Best" and "worst" are legitimate extremes in grammar, but the way we apply those contradictory terms may be simplistic. That depends on how extreme are the views we hold. It is more effective for the judgments we make to realize that something may still occur that is better or worse at some time. "Always" and "never" represent the extremes of the stability that we so much desire. Yet even though process is something we don't want to face much of the time, it is incumbent upon us to adjust our mindset and expression to that normal state of the world.

CHAPTER 6

Objectivity:
The Elusive Goal

s there a golden mean that we can strike between polar extremes? If there is, no matter how broad it must be, how can we know how objective our judgments or those of others are? Most of us aren't scholars or pundits, and even if we were, we wouldn't have all the facts, nor would we necessarily have the only correct opinion. What standards can there be for "objectivity"?

The narrow, simplest meaning of the word evokes the scientist's view: seeing something for its physically observable (and measurable) properties, uninfluenced by the viewer's biases or perceptual limitations. It is that latter phrase that is most pertinent here.

If we really want to be objective, or think that we are, we have to look into ourselves with diligence and honesty. We have to really want to do that and to be willing. What really are our motives in sticking to a particular view? We may not always be aware of them. What are our biases, which we have to keep digging deeper into the sub-basement of our psyche for? Biases themselves can prevent us from seeing through them. But at least we ought to get into the habit of asking ourselves what intellectual or perceptual biases we may have. Are we prepared to examine the opposite or the alternative to our views? Do we examine contexts, or are we reluctant to see them because to do so would cause us to give up an idea we held earlier or had expressed publicly? Also to be asked of ourselves: Are we apt to form premature judgments?

Humility also plays a part. We ought never to assume that we have all the necessary facts for an eternal opinion. Obviously, to come to decisions for some pending action, we have to act on the facts we have and on the judgments we've made. But we have to reserve some intellectual space for saying, "This is the best I can do now, but perhaps other facts may come up later that may cause me to change my evaluation."

All of this is hard to do. The inputs to our subjectivity subtly interfere with the objectivity we're aiming for. It is hard to see beyond our frame of reference, as the next chapter will show.

It's also hard to get rid of first impressions. A person's appearance, dress, demeanor, speech, and voice can turn us off or on. So can knowledge of their education, experience, cultural background, accomplishments, reputation, and status. These kinds of characteristics might tend to bias a scientist's expectations or even his choices of parameters in an experiment, but they would wither away in face of evidence and the disciplines of investigation.

And what of words themselves? How objectively are they used? Words of extravagant degree (e.g., stupendous, outrageous, tyrannical, satanic) may be used undeservedly to bias our opinion. Euphemisms (Greek for "good words"), such as *pre-owned* instead of *used* and so on, are meant to reduce negative images or to obfuscate. Strung out into one-line blurbs for films—"Best this year," (offered in March!), adoring comments on book jackets, and so on—are the norm. We may know they are hyperbole, but are influenced by them nonetheless. These techniques of advertising continually push the limits not only of objectivity but of ethics and legality.

As commercialized forms of influence, they stand somewhere between persuasion as a legitimate art and propaganda. The latter, in its commonly accepted pejorative sense, could be called an illegitimate art, perhaps "improperganda"!

This is nothing new, however highly developed in our own time. Persuasion techniques have been developed and refined ever since the days of the ancient Greeks. The sophists of Socrates' time, sought to teach wisdom through argumentation. But they sincerely felt that no objective truth could be arrived at. Socrates took issue with this belief, using persuasive argumentation as a means of searching for truth. The sophists, moreover, spawned a cadre of paid wordsmiths who used clever wording and even fallacious reasoning to persuade the listener to a preferred viewpoint. So has sophistry come to mean clever but phony argument?

Aristotle, the father of rhetoric, developed its fine points with the purpose of overcoming this degraded argumentation. He established devices that would permit one to distinguish between the merely colorful, invalid argumentation and ethical, valid reasoning as a means of seeking the truth. So elaborate was his system, however, that it was easily corrupted by miscomprehension, or by being turned into a facile technique. Rhetoric, consequently, has long since taken on the connotation of subjective verbiage that masks the truth.

At the other pole from true rhetoric is propaganda. Since volumes have been written about each, there is no need to spend much space on them here. What characterizes propaganda today is its intent to deceive. This implies a built-in difficulty in detecting it, especially when the latter is subtle. Unfortunately, even as we may hold a cynical attitude about what politicians tell us, we often do not apply that skepticism to the specifics of what we are told. Nor are we able to separate the truth from the fiction.

Most people want to believe the established authorities and sources of information. It is easier to do so, and we need to have faith in such monuments of society. They act as surrogate parents that we all desire.

The aural and visual media of the twentieth century gave us the blatant, dramatic huckstering of the Hitler, Mussolini, or Stalin era. But techniques like the big lie, stupendous ceremonies to make the bosom swell with pride, character assassination, and inducing paranoia can sway each new generation. People who may see through such bombast are vulnerable to new techniques, however. The term "disinformation" has entered our language. Given in small doses (as in short sound bites on TV), repeated endlessly, presented as broad generalizations to the exclusion of pertinent facts, claimed as complete coverage, and associated with a desired mood, they can easily influence us. "What are a speaker's motivations, goals, gains, or losses in saying what he or she does?" we have to ask.

In wars as the worst case, the populace is denied objectivity by what the government tells us. Commission of outright lies, omission of facts, exaggeration, and innuendo are all used. Miscalculations by statesmen or generals about the battle of Gallipoli in World War I and in the Gulf of Tonkin episode in the Viet Nam war, for example, are not revealed, if at all, till decades later. Our losses are minimized and our victories trumpeted, often prematurely, as are the enemy's defeats.

Governments are notorious in using these techniques in times of social or economic distress. Extreme characterizations are used to arouse anger and fear. Suspicions are planted about evil forces aligned against us, the eternal "red herring" of the infidel in the Crusades or the Communists of the twentieth century.

Associating ideas with icons of credibility, such as authority figures or popular people, is a hallmark for advertising and propaganda. Conversely, name-calling, negative stereotyping, and innuendos about political or sexual orientation are also typical techniques. These appeals to personal attributes are *ad hominem* fallacies.

Fallacies are another subject on which many books have been written, so there is no need to dwell on them except to note them as examples of a mode of thought. They are apt to be the result of shoddy thinking and can be consciously used by clever persuaders to obscure, diminish, or emphasize an idea or point of view. Because they involve apparent connections (as of cause and effect, use of age as status symbol, etc.), they are compelling. It is easy to fail to see that each fallacy represents faulty logic.

Allied to the "post hoc" fallacy are illogical or extravagant predictions. Here the ordinary person is at the mercy of the Chicken Little "The sky is falling!" scare, because of the fear aroused and the likelihood that one can't appropriately analyze the factors involved. Of course, powerful factions may have the ability to cause such fears to come true in order to prove their power and credibility. The Nazis' setting the Reichstag building on fire as "proof" of the threat of Communists in their midst is a classic example.

Another technique worth mentioning because it is sly is to get the audience to accept what is said by obligating or embarrassing them. Remarks such as, "It is obvious that . . ." or "Anyone can tell that . . ." may be used to make people feel stupidly undiscerning, nonconformist, or unpatriotic.

The Scientists' Mode

All the exploitation of words described above is the antithesis of the way language is used for scientific objectivity. What does the scientific style of thinking offer as a model?

Objectivity is the unquestioned premise of any scientific evaluation. It is intrinsic to the nature of instruments and measurement and to the rock of evidence upon which science is anchored. So, first, opinions have to be supported by hard evidence. Presumably, if a scientist describes what he or she sees by aided or unaided eye or by a meter or other indirect reading, he or she is reporting a true fact. Yet we know that, despite this guiding principle, visual or other sensual perceptions may be limited in some ways, as may be instrumental readings. Instrumental readings may be biased by inherent characteristics of the instrument, and experimental investigations may be skewed by the design of the experiment.

In science, these sources of bias or error are counteracted as much as possible by the techniques of replication of a given experiment, by attempts to achieve the same result through different experimental designs, and by peer review. These techniques are both proactive and reactive for checking objectivity. As procedures, these are not so different from what the diligent layman goes through in forming an evaluation. We reinforce initial opinions with additional facts, we may check our facts from various sources, and we may bounce our ideas off of other people who may challenge us. But for the scientist, there is more than technique at work.

Second, there is attitude. By virtue of the time and effort involved, the thoroughness of getting the facts requires restraint and patience in making judgments. These are the temperaments that many people lack when making their judgments, as they are not under the constraints of the protocols of scientists. Also, the spur-of-the-moment timing of giving an opinion may not be conducive to deliberative judgments.

Tentativity or skepticism in accepting evaluations is at least a tacit attitude. These attitudes imply what the general semanticists call "semantic relaxation"—avoiding impulsive judgments. Training ourselves to adopt such a frame of mind will free us to substitute questioning and imaginative brainstorming. Are we being told everything that is pertinent? What are the short—or long-term implications of what we see or are being told? What are the alternatives or the opposites of what is being presented? What factors led to this evidence?

As an example, think how we might evaluate information about poverty and welfare. Both are generally decried. But we reify them as generalized abstractions and frequently have knee-jerk, conventional assumptions about people involved with them: They "are lazy and/or conditioned to expectations of handouts." Less often do we seek out or keep in mind the operational realities. These may include poor education, poor self-esteem, frustration, hopelessness, or bitterness. These characteristics make it difficult for these people to get jobs. Because they don't have jobs, they are in a position to be tarred with the very characterizations we identify them with. A self-fulfilling prophecy comes true: The characteristics that we identify these people with after the fact are ascribed as the causes.

It is tough for the average person to dig for this information or to keep it at his fingertips. I am merely pointing out the differences in thinking between what the ordinary person and the one with a scientific mindset has been trained to do.

Quantification is part of the language of the scientific mindset, though even numerical data has to be scrutinized. So professional wordsmiths—editors, reviewers, textbook evaluators, and others—have attempted to objectify what is written or said with numerical techniques. In speech or text, the number of different types of words (active and passive verbs, personal pronouns, etc.), the average number and length of words in a sentence, the number of sentences in a paragraph, and so on, will be counted. Various formulae have been developed to relate the numbers of each category. The final score is placed within various classes of style or readability.

Reliance primarily on the grammatical forms of words does not give a good indication of more qualitative content, such as the cognitive or substantive content or the viewpoint of the communication. These formulae are a good try, but they throw the ball of objectivity back into the court of the observer's subjective criteria.

A closer approach to the qualitative aspects is attempted by Content Analysis. This has been used extensively to analyze television programs. Here the analysts try to systematize what a "normally intelligent" person would do in forming an evaluation as to the criteria they use; for example, tallying the number of times that references are made to some characteristic of interest, such as personality types, values, or ideas.

This technique is also a good attempt at giving an objective evaluation of a text (written or spoken). Such analyses are inevitably limited by the analysts' frame of reference goals, biases, and so on, as well as by the obvious looseness and subjectivity of the parameters. They are as close as one can get to a work that does not, after all, involve hard evidence. With the latter, a scientist doesn't have such problems. He or she can describe a work with terminology defined by demonstrable functions or operations.

We are probably all familiar with surveys used by legislators, political campaign managers, news media, and commercial enterprises taking the pulse of their readers. Respondents have to be acute in reading the way questions are phrased in the hope that they will lead to objective assessments of the constituencies' opinions.

Since the major source of opinions and facts are the news media, journalists have long been in the forefront of those for whom objectivity has been a goal and ethic. We are accustomed to the realization that news media have at least a subtle bias. Their departure from objectivity is excused under the elegant rubric of "editorial policy."

Various professional media organizations have codes of ethics, which include criteria for objectivity. These involve giving attribution of sources; labeling content as to degree of facts, secondhand opinion, or rumor; identifying editorial content as distinct from reportage; using bylines for feature writers who give their own opinions: checking other sources for facts; and providing opportunity for presentation of opposing views, among others. Still, objectivity can only be a goal.

These canons fulfill the witnesses' oath and provide peer review, all in keeping with scientific canons. Scientific and scholarly journals may be stricter than the news media in carrying out these precepts, since their articles have to pass the gates not merely of editors but of a panel of experts. Scholarly reports keep factual matters separate from opinions, and the discussion section of reports help to give balanced viewpoints.

Summary

Objectivity requires that facts presented have to be as sufficient and correct as possible, and that they are required to be clearly separate from opinion. Both need to be as free as possible from perceptual or other biases or at least these should be acknowledged. Sources of information also should be acknowledged. Because objectivity cannot be measured as definitively as scientific evidence, it pays to be alert and discerning about the subtle manipulation of words from those with axes to grind.

The elusive nature of objectivity can be a hurdle to realizing some of the inputs to our outputs of communication. Perhaps the hardest thing to realize about what affects the opinions we hold and the evaluations we express is the frame of reference in which we organize our impressions and conclusions. That is the subject of the next chapter.

CHAPTER 7

Frames of Reference:
Mayan Hieroglyphics, Adolescent Stress,
and More

For many years, Mayan hieroglyphics were interpreted by several noted experts as showing that those pre-Columbian people had a peaceful, pastoral culture. Their reputation was such that successive researchers were lulled into perceiving the same scene or story in undeciphered glyphs. Interpretations that did not fit the accepted theories were disregarded.

When a later researcher was bold enough to give a different interpretation to the glyphs, however, a diametrically opposed picture emerged from the very same carvings. What had previously been seen as pastoral activity was now seen to reveal a culture that engaged in gruesome mutilation.

Consider, too, that in studies of adolescent stress (described by Andrea Brooks in a *New York Times* article of Nov. 29, 1983) teachers and psychologists gave different rankings than did teenage boys. Dropping out of school was considered by the scholastically oriented professionals to be much more stressful for young people than it was to the teenagers themselves.

Both of these examples illustrate how one's frame of reference, even within the same subject areas, can produce contradictory results. The somewhat arcane example of the hieroglyphs is from anthropology, a subject that attempts to gain insights about modern cultures by studying those of the past. Here is a case where many of the same engravings, in a matter that would hardly be biased by current social issues, could be ambiguously interpreted. The more pragmatic and urgent example of adolescent stress relates to a condition that has led to tragic suicides on the part of young people at an age when their behavior is perplexing to them and troubling to adults.

Both cases demonstrate the grip that a frame of reference can have. The failure to see beyond one's own frame of reference is one of the biggest sources of trouble in reaching wise or efficient solutions to problems. In evaluating observations and forming opinions, it can blind a person to the other person's point of view. It can bias even the scholars' research—the data sought, the methods chosen, the interpretations made, and the conclusions drawn.

It is as if a person were to view a complex painting through a small frame exposing only a limited area. One might then tend to focus on the details, which would be relatively prominent, but one would describe the picture only from that one segment. Conversely, viewing the whole painting from a distance would prevent an appreciation of the details.

This brings up the matter of relativism—seeing your views in relation to a wider context or to alternative viewpoints. The general semanticists call this "extensionalizing." It evokes Einstein's concept discussed in Chapter 1. Some critics feel that a relativist view would lead to not upholding any particular values or to not taking a firm stand on an issue. That is not so. Relativism does not mean having both feet planted firmly in mid-air, nor does it mean that one set of values is necessarily as good as another.

What it does mean is that, in forming an opinion, a person will not have done so from a narrow, parochial standpoint. One may not agree with another person's values, but one has to acknowledge their possible validity. It implies that one is at least able to see another person's views or values from that person's standpoint. Nothing less should be required of mature, intelligent, open-minded people.

The inputs one chooses in forming an opinion are often affected, however unconsciously, by the values involved. Customarily, we look at a situation only from the vantage point we are most familiar with or the one we prefer—at least initially. We do so even more spontaneously and strongly if we feel emotional about the matter or have some vested interest in it. So it pays to ask ourselves what our orientation is and what values are involved compared to some other presentation of opinion.

Admittedly, it is difficult to see many viewpoints as if from on-high. We usually don't have the necessary knowledge. This goes without saying, but too often we act as though this were not so. It's a good habit, then, to remind ourselves of this reality as a prompt to putting ourselves into the other person's shoes.

Why discuss something so obvious? Unfortunately, in real-life situations, it is too often not obvious that this is happening. A dramatic example of a reminder to adopt another frame of reference was spelled out with tragic results in the Challenger space shuttle disaster of 1986.

The vice president for engineering of Morton Thiokol Company, arguing that the shuttle launch be delayed because seals between the rocket sections were not considered to be reliable in the cold weather, was reminded by the senior vice president, "Put on your management hat." Undoubtedly, each man was *capable* of seeing the other's viewpoint once the pertinent facts were on the table. What was really at issue was the weight that was to be given to one point of view over the other. That part of decision-making involves a higher level of assessment in which relative values do come into play. But the senior vice president's remark implied that the other man's outlook was too parochial and that he did not evaluate the launching relative to other important viewpoints.

A standard tenet of scientific thinking is that theory has to fit the facts, not the reverse. In truth, however, the temptation to interpret some evidence so that it fits into a pet theory can come from a desire to keep consistency in the theory. This brings up the problem of completion and consistency that was seen in Kurt Goedel's quest.for completeness or consistency.

A certain tolerance exists for bits of evidence that don't fit the scheme and that keep the theory from being complete, as it is assumed that this evidence can be explained at a later date. This is especially true for theoretical models that don't lend themselves to experimental manipulation, as would be the case in astronomy or anthropology. At some point, the accumulation of evidence that doesn't fit the theory readily or at all will tip the balance. But the judgment about when this weight is great enough is again subject to the frame of reference of the evaluators.

The tendency to make the facts fit the theory can become an obsession if a person is driven by ideology to the exclusion of practicality in some degree. In the case of social or international tension, under the heat of threats real or perceived, it is easy for political leaders to distill complex situations, condensing them with simplistic rhetoric to fit the ideology they think or want to have people believe. The one-sided viewpoint of the common man, thus induced, becomes the narrow frame of reference of a nation. This is absorbed by even sophisticated and knowledgeable people who are, after all, prisoners of their own egos, drives, insecurities and mindsets, not to mention the information available, and who may not be noted for wisdom.

In such manner, major military losses have occurred, suffered by leaders who had studied previous wars but could not get beyond the assumptions that were their reference points. The red coats worn proudly and conventionally by the British, which left them visible to Indian fighters in the French and Indian War, had their updated version in the heavy arms of the Americans that were no match for bamboo spikes and other guerrilla tactics in Viet Nam two hundred years later. Other examples were the fortress mentality that built the Maginot Line breached by Hitler and the assumptions by some in 1941 that "little" Japan could not or would not attack the United States.

In the potentially explosive world of international relations that existed between the US and the former USSR—the prime contenders in the twentieth century—each move was explained from opposing frames of reference. Thus, what the Western powers justified in their 1919 occupation of northern Russia, the Soviets saw as reason for their continuing suspicions. What the West considered to be the reprehensible Nazi-Soviet Non-Aggression Pact of 1939, the Soviets viewed as a prudent forestalling of an invasion by the Germans that would have had the tacit blessings of western European nations.

In these major events of history each side may well have misunderstood the other's frame of reference. Pragmatic, strategic interests of each were at work. On a deeper level was an unwillingness or inability to credit the validity of the opponent's view of those facts based upon his orientation. This level amounts to mindset. Subsequent chapters will attempt to shine some light into this basement of our thinking structure.

These dynamics exist in less dramatic issues between smaller groups and between individuals, who can truly be compared to horses with blinders charging into battle. In any week, one can read in the newspapers about an individual or group of people on one side of an issue who complain that the opinions expressed or actions taken by the other side failed to show recognition of the first group's point of view. Workers who perceive a need for benefits that their employers feel are not their due; people on welfare from poverty or some kind of disability whom the politicians or the financially comfortable consider lazy and undeserving; and people of color and other minorities, who see subtle forms of discrimination acting against them that the ethnic majority have no inkling of . . . The issues are legion.

The inertia of the frame of reference by which each side justifies its actions becomes a built-in drive to ignore a relativist view even when a lessening of tensions occurs. The emotions have been aroused, and positions have been expressed and rationalized from which it would be too great a blow to the ego or reputation to withdraw. Our sense of security is bolstered by this attitude reinforcement.

This seems to be a normal, even if undesirable, response from most of us. Our intellect takes a back seat to our fight-or-flight responses. Therefore, we tend not to ask ourselves if we are presenting our presumably dependable facts and our strongly preferred arguments from a particular frame of reference. Even if we were to recognize this situation intellectually, we might not be able or willing to step outside of ourselves to examine what the frame of reference is. We may not recognize what our premises are; or if we do, we may not be willing to change them.

One might expect that intelligent people of goodwill would consciously and actively see where the other party is coming from. Without their experience or responsibilities, however, this is hard to do.

Most people aren't conditioned to automatically seek the other viewpoint. This relates to self-protection, but also to considerateness as a style. Yet, just as a military party needs to understand its adversary, a person of a more mature mentality realizes that his self-defense is improved if he understands his opponent's motives and aims, understanding an adversary's reference frame as a first step. Quite apart from empathy, this could avoid tensions and lead to wiser, more positive responses.

These nostrums may seem too simple to be worth much in the real world of hard knocks. They foresee an ideal, rational world, which the human animal is probably only groping toward. But that is what the average person yearns for and science aims for.

Five W's and One H Again

Can we consciously speed up the process? Can we step outside of our frame of reference to see things in a relativistic manner? Is this not the problem Heisenberg's Principle implies and that Goedel said we could never solve—that as products of a system, we can't examine that system?

Fortunately, human affairs have flexibility, unlike physical phenomena. We can move to many reference points within them for judging our own position.

Indeed, in the last half of the twentieth century, popular techniques have been developed for doing this. Role-playing has become a standard device for teaching and therapy. Brainstorming—developing creative, unconventional ideas by randomly throwing mental darts—is used in business meetings, seminars, and corporate "think-tanks."

How, then, can we learn to step outside of ourselves? Tnree things are needed. First, we have to be sensitive to the general problem that we all have a frame of reference and that our viewpoint is not the only correct, objective, or fair one. Second, we have to develop a recognition that the other person's reference frame can be as valid as ours so that we adopt a *willingness* to see "where his head is at." Finally, we have to seek the particular components of our viewpoint, our premises and their sources, and we have to be aware of what the components of others' frames of reference may be.

Seeing these prescripts in print, we can agree to them, and it may seem ridiculous to have to spell them out. But habitual insensitivity may not match what we admit to intellectually in particular situations. Subtle and complex emotional and cultural biases are at work. That is why it is important to have people from different ethnic, cultural, and religious backgrounds participate in decision-making in social programs, as mere possession of certain facts will not suffice.

Nor do obvious determinants, such as age and sex, education and financial status. Psychological aspects operate. These include our goals versus those of others. These may be pragmatic, as with buyers versus sellers, manufacturers versus users; they may involve a hierarchy of authority, such as boss/employee, parent/child, or teacher/student. Professional expertise and standards of quality as well as ethical and moral values may enter.

Still deeper are aspects that touch on our view of ourselves, and those that trigger the emotions. Psychologists tell us that most people tend to assess situations with themselves as the focal point. They see themselves incorrectly as the butt of a joke, take criticism too much to heart even though the critic may be wrong, or see themselves as more important to a situation than they really are.

We may have hidden cravings for ego-satisfying one-upmanship in terms of money, position, reputation, or adulation. We may have built-in insecurities about absorbing ideas that are different, challenging, or threatening. Even scientists may not be above such human drives as some notorious hoaxes and falsifications demonstrate.

There is no specific scientific model for choosing a frame of reference. But there are some practical questions we can ask to analyze the one we have. Learning to ask them systematically is where the scientists' training, aptitudes, and attitudes come into play.

The proper guides are the five W's and one H that a good reporter must consider: who, what, when, where, why, and how. Not all of these may be pertinent, but one ought to ask oneself if they are. (This harkens back to Chapter 2.)

A cognitive dynamic also has to be applied. That is, one must think for each of these questions, "What are the alternatives?" These may be opposites (absence instead of presence, increase instead of decrease, etc.); they may be different in kind; they may differ in degree; or they may include additional examples. Also, how may each of these aspects change, and at what rate? Social conditions or an individual's outlook may be changing by such small increments as to be imperceptible or they may not be perceived by some who are not watching acutely so that a simmering change becomes apparent only when it boils over, too late to prevent it. People who note tiny changes may see them only as isolated events, failing to synthesize them into a larger significance.

Most people undoubtedly run through some of these possibilities, but at random. The scientific mindset (though not necessarily only the scientist) would follow these procedures more purposefully and more systematically.

A prime example of this type of thinking among scientists is Einstein's bold explanation for the results of the Michaelson-Morely experiments about the speed of light. In that case, the "what" of the frame of reference was the ether, whose existence virtually everyone accepted. By contrast to its presence, Einstein's alternative was to posit its absence.[4]

Coming down to earth, a pragmatic example of increase yielding to its opposite in the viewpoint of researchers is given by experiments in the use of the metal boron to harden steel. This was a most important goal in the

---

4   Ernst Mach, whose name is associated with the speed of sound, felt that these experiments confirmed his own earlier belief that there was no ether.

era of World War II when other alloying elements used for this purpose were in short supply. Here the frame of reference for the "how" of boron use was to parallel the way carbon (to which it is similar) was added: to try increasing amounts from some chosen starting point. This kept failing to show desired results. Finally, some experimenter realized that the tacit assumption of "more is better" was heading in the wrong direction—a decrease was necessary! Ultimately the required amount was lowered to 0.001 percent.

An example of going beyond a frame of reference by adding a possibility illustrates alternatives that differ in kind, at least as a variation of an existing concept. This comes from a challenge to Euclid's geometry. Since about 300 BC, people had used his rules to describe space in three dimensions by which we know it. In the mid-nineteenth century, several mathematicians attacked the least certain of his axioms: that only one parallel line could be drawn through a point outside of a straight line. But did one *know* that two such lines could never meet? These men posed the impertinent question, What kind of geometry would result if there could be more than one such line?

This might seem a ridiculous question for practical purposes, but mathematicians think in an open-ended way. Their approach was theoretical. Given the abstract nature of mathematics as a language, one can manipulate symbols arbitrarily if one chooses to speculate. For example, as radius "a" can be described for its position relative to the three axes by $x^2 + y^2 + z^2 + = a^2$. But one could arbitrarily write $x^2 + y^2 + z^2 + m^2 + n^2 = b^2$ and see what happens if we tried to solve that equation if it had more than three dimensions. In this manner, Bernhard Riemann extended the reasoning that questions Euclid's axioms by positing a geometry equation based on the fact that *no* parallel lines could pass through the point outside the straight line. His conceptualization of multidimensional geometry languished for several decades as an academic curiosity. Then came Einstein's concept of four dimensions of space and time. Riemann's non-Euclidean formulation provided very neatly the mathematics needed to describe it.

Beyond its scientific usefulness, its exemplary imaginativeness lay in the fact that Riemann (and his predecessors in related work) freed himself not only from conventional thinking—specifically, of rectangular coordinates—but from the very idea of tying their speculations to the frame of reference of physical reality.

How do these patterns for the lofty world of arcane scientific subjects apply to daily human interactions?

Take a simple common situation: Someone may not hear from a friend about an anticipated get-together. Most of us would wonder why, and several possibilities might immediately come to mind. However, many people tend to see themselves as at the center of events. So they may simply be annoyed and not follow up the incident. They may feel the other person has the first obligation to call, overlooking that the other person may have tried to reach them several times while they were out. Or they may take offense at what seems to be a slight, and even become angry. In this way do small rebuffs grow into huge hatred.

Such a self-centered frame of reference inhibits the kind of response where we *automatically* think of alternatives. More systematic speculations might go something like this: *Who* is involved? Could another person have affected our plans or the friend's response? Who might that be? *What* could be her reasons for failing to respond? She might be ill, she could have had an emergency, she could have changed her mind and neglected to call. *When* was she supposed to call? Did I get the date wrong? When might she have called without finding me home? *Where* could she be? Perhaps she had to go away, for any number of reasons. *How* can I resolve the situation? By waiting, by calling, by writing? A habitually open-minded empathic attitude would be apt to consider these alternatives right away.

As to thinking in terms of opposites, take the case of a student who does poorly in school. Parents and teachers notoriously view such young people, from unruly kindergarteners through college drop-outs, as rebellious or lazy, or think, "Kids have no respect these days!" But adults' views may be dimmed by the soft focus of their own idealized behavior. Their imperfect recollections are poor criteria for measuring today's behavior.

In pondering the causes or cures for the younger person's attitude, adults might ask, "Is this rebellious attitude only the other side of suppressed creative energy?" Is the "laziness" a lack of motivation from a humdrum environment? Instances of brilliant achievers who did poorly in high school because they found it dull are legendary. Aggravated parents and jaded teachers may not be conditioned to think in terms of seeking explanations that may be 180 degrees from their peremptory judgments.

Such a reversal of direction should also be applied to *who*, those in the student's life who play a part in these behaviors. Usually, friends are blamed. But what about the opposite end of his social spectrum. What about the teachers who the student habitually blames and therefore seems to be exonerated by the adults? What about the parents themselves?

Daring to ask these questions would then open up one's thinking to additional or alternative sources for the unacceptable behavior. *What* situations tend to produce these behaviors? How did they come about? *When* were they first noticed? *Where* did these operate—at home, in school, with particular groups of people?

Probably most parents do fulfill these injunctions to fine-tune their thinking, but too many react in a self-defensive, reflexive, habitual, or rigid way. The patience, persistence, and imaginativeness of the scientist's habit of digging deeper is lacking.

The differences in frame of reference show in many scenarios that we are all familiar with: the parent wishing to offer guidance and the child wanting to assert his or her independence; the new bride with her mother-in-law. We react like the little child whose toy is taken by another who only wants to hold it or join in play. These responses keep us from receiving what might be entirely opposite interpretations, for example, a parent or in-law leaning over backward, not wanting to interfere, may be seen as uncaring or resentful. Similarly, one trying to be helpful can be perceived as blocking the younger person's initiative. In this way, we create the very situations that we observe. The source of misunderstanding thus conveyed can be as hard to pinpoint as the position of an electron in its mobile quantum states.

In these "measurements" of social, political, and economic matters, we are most vulnerable to frame of reference. With our pocketbooks at stake in issues like the stock market, jarred by news of environmental damage or by the constant din about international threats, it is easy to form instant "analyses."

Flooded with sources of information today, we have ample opportunities for getting others' views and giving our own, e.g., letters to the editor, TV and radio talk shows and call-ins, and Internet chat rooms. These outlets, accessible to most of us, take time, interest, and probity. So we may not bother to read beyond the lead paragraph that sums up who, what, when, and where, but often does not include why. Many issues are presented in the media with the storytelling simplicity of medieval stained-glass windows, so we may miss the shadings.

Nor can most of use do the kind of research that a scholar or scientist would invest in learning about a subject. Most people haven't been trained to be *instinctively* analytical, although analysis in the media abound.

Because our reference points for forming judgments may be vague, shifting, and self-serving, the simple, one-sided evaluation fits most readily into our prior attitudes. It is easier for us to push our own view, aware that the other guy will push his. Thus our initial response becomes our final one, leading to a hardening of the attitudes. Tuning out instead of fine-tuning, we then become more confrontational.

Our Premises: The Silent Conspirators

Endless facts, pro and con, can be adduced to support an opinion, and one could never make headway against all the points and counterpoints. But there is a deeper fund of inputs to our frame of reference: our premises. They are a much harder source to seek out and to change, as they blend into what constitutes mindset.

We are so conditioned by our upbringing, education, and social environment to what is conventional and acceptable that it never occurs to most of us to ask what our basic assumptions are or to question whether they are correct. Certainly most people, even great thinkers, have steered clear of thinking, or proclaiming, what might be considered heresy.

That is not supposed to be the mode of science, however much it may have been the pattern of all-too-human scientists. Perhaps Galileo is the most well-known of the latter. The ideal scientific mind is always aware that accepted theories may be overthrown. As new evidence accumulates, there is a virtual professional mandate to challenge the accepted wisdom. The challenge may be resisted strongly, of course, on professional grounds of demanding more evidence or on psychological grounds of egos and reputations.

In some of the examples cited above, premises were challenged or left untouched. Those that were disputed did not spring up spontaneously. Goedel challenged the idea of consistency and completeness because of a prior search for their combination, just as Einstein was led to challenge the idea of the ether because of examining the evidence in light of its assumed existence. With the Challenger, the premise of safety as a top priority was matched against those of pragmatism and expediency. The

Mayan scholars' earlier interpretations were premised on the rectitude of earlier scholars.

Such assumptions may be those of classes or people or whole societies, not just of individuals. On the international scale of military fiascos, as on the interpersonal scale surrounding the case of teenagers' stress, one may suspect that assumptions of status, conventionality, and others were left unexamined. In evaluations by an older generation, the tendency to assume superiority of wisdom or authority is very great and in some societies unquestioned.

Summary

To sum up, we need to be sensitive to the fact that we each have a frame of reference in making evaluations that we may not be aware of. The Theories of Relativity and Uncertainty are paradigms for this awareness. They imply reference points shifting in time and space and alert us to think with relativism and to be aware of the effects we may produce on the very thing we observe. The examples cited to illustrate these points have been mundane precisely to show how these principles can be used to analyze ordinary situations.

The attitudes that underlie our premises come from complex, usually unconscious patterns tied to our values and our self-image. But what impels us to choose a particular stance for viewing a situation? What leads us to place the frame over a particular area? Two hidden forces, one given by nature and one by civilization, are at work, as the next two chapters will relate.

PART II

INPUTS

CHAPTER 8

Perceptions and Misperceptions

D o we really see what we think we see, or hear what we think we hear? Our frame of reference is on the cusp of the outputs of our evaluations—what we think and say—and of the inputs—our physical perceptions. So it would be helpful to look at how the latter operate, and then link these inputs by analogies to a frame of reference. When we see something or perceive it by any other sense, we usually have an immediate idea of what our senses have conveyed. At the instant, however, we undoubtedly don't realize all that our minds are taking into account to form that idea. We are unaware of built-in biases. What we perceive as sensations has been colored by experiences that have been associated with them since birth.

So what are these goings-on that color what we see? (By "see" I mean "comprehension," not simply optical sensation.)

Paying Attention

First, we must give our attention to something, as the farmer explained to a visitor who was astonished to see him hit his supposedly intelligent goat over the head with a two-by-four, "You have to get his attention first." That is, we must be *ready to attend.* Everyone no doubt has had the experience of being preoccupied, tired, uninterested, or distracted so that they fail to hear or see some event or detail.

Once we are ready to attend, a myriad of selectivities comes into play.

Selective attention governs the specific things that we pay attention to. Many things can steer us in this may: Our mind may be on another matter; something may catch our eye or act in the background; or there may be a subliminal perception of something we like or dislike, such as a subtle fragrance or sound.

Selective exposure comes from our preferences and biases. Our needs may lead us to seek out only certain sectors of our surroundings. Most of us tend to read those newspapers, listen to those programs, go to those meetings, and associate with those people who we already agree with. It is intellectually tiring, uncomfortable, and possibly unnerving to spend time listening to an opposing viewpoint. This shortchanges us intellectually by denying us necessary materials for forming intelligent evaluations.

Once we do allow ourselves to come into contact with a situation, we still may miss some important aspects. We tend to hear what we want to hear and to see what we expect to see. Think of the wife who may say to her husband (or the parent to a child) in annoyance, "You only hear what you want to hear!" This *selective perception* is one side of the coin; the fact is that we may not remember what was unpleasant or contrary to our views. *Selective memory* then can be the source of still another accusation. *Selective retention* and *selective recall* are additional filters. Even though information may be in our memory bank, we have not programmed ourselves to retrieve it. The reasons again are many: lack of contact with the information (which may increase with age), lack of interest, attempts to repress the information from fear or guilt, and so on.

These psychological factors come into play notoriously with witnesses to an accident or a crime. It is because of these acknowledged deficiencies that lawyers for opposing sides frequently seek to undermine the credibility of witnesses. Similarly, identification of potential offenders in a police lineup can be made incorrectly because of these subtle contributors to visual perception.

Our ability to evaluate is therefore affected in the first instance by this normal tendency of our minds to select only certain aspects of the subject at hand. As a result, a person who is unaware of this may fail to see how his preference to see things from a certain point of view is warped by these fundamental limitations.

Grouping

Once we have perceived something, our minds try to organize the observation to group or contrast it with other observations. In this way, the endless impressions that bombard us can be dealt with more easily. This enhances our security, for, at base, it involves a survival function. By associating similar characteristics, we can locate the source of sustenance and predict probable risks and outcomes.

Organization involves three essential modes. The first is making sense of incomplete data, so as to identify an object or situation. The second is seeing the thing or event in relation to its surroundings, and the third depends upon that relationship. By comparing and contrasting with the surrounding objects or events, we evaluate and classify the observation as unique or part of a larger, more familiar group.

The first mode is concerned with wholeness, so our filling in of missing information leads to *closure.* The other two modes relate to proximity in two respects: in terms of spatial distance and in terms of closeness of characteristics. This qualitative proximity lets us form named classifications. These modes of closure, proximity, and context have been elucidated by the Gestalt psychologists, who made great contributions to understanding the perceptual inputs to our evaluations.

Closure is the easiest of the three modes to grasp and is the minimum requirement for forming an opinion and for making later comparisons. Without closure for identification, any evaluation would be fuzzy. In Fig. 5, the discontinuities in the picture of the hat and the cross illustrate how we deal with perceptions of things that are not "closed."

Fig. 5. HAT AND CROSS

We are left with a vague feeling of discomfort, consciously or not. From our knowledge of common objects, and possibly because of a kind of visual momentum or logic, our mind's eye tends to join the discontinuous lines or spaces if we are given enough clues to start with. An apparent lack of closure may well be a factor in our response to abstract or other forms of modern art.

The objects in Fig.5 are visual analogs for perceptions by our other senses that have been conditioned by experience, such as an unresolved musical harmony, even unseasoned food. Analogies with the sense of touch and smell would be more tenuous to make.

They can also be made on the level of intellect, for example, in reading a story that has no conclusion or listening to reasoning that has no logical resolution. Some of us, of course, catch on quicker than others, as in doing crossword puzzles.

A most important example of closure in communication is in giving *feedback*. When one does not respond to a communication, it is not merely a discourtesy or inefficiency but a failure to satisfy this need for closure. A simple "thank you" is functionally an acknowledgment of the completion of the circuit. A more substantive acknowledgement may be warranted.

Premature closure can occur when a person jumps to conclusions. This is akin to a child's desire for instant gratification. In a sense, this is not true closure because the presentation of all the necessary facts is not completed before the observer forms his opinion. When we succumb to the selectivities discussed above, we are also victims, however unconsciously, of incomplete closure.

So from the simple visual perceptions to the most complex intellectual ones, there is a human drive and ability to attain closure. The fact that we frequently do so prematurely or simplistically is a big stumbling block to making sound evaluations.

Proximity and similarity. Once we have identified an object, person, or situation, memory and recall lead to comparing it with similar objects and then to their context. Figs. 6a and 6b illustrate the effects of spatial context.

Figs 6a and 6b Perspectives

Figs. 6a and 6b illustrate spatial context. In 6a. cylinders of equal height appear to be different in height because of contextual location; in 6b, figures that might have the same height appear different because of proximity to the viewer.

The ambiguity that can enter into purely visual inputs is seen in the often published "face/vase" or "figure/ground" image of Fig.7.

Fig.7 Ambiguous Images: Context-Object Relationship

Which is context, which is object? Perceived figure (vase or faces) depends upon frame of reference chosen by observer.

Even more ambiguous is the "witch/maid" in Fig. 8.

Fig. 8 Ambiguity within an Object
Is this a picture of a young girl or of an old woman?

Some abstract diagrams for these concepts will probably be helpful for illustrating the purely sensory reactions as well as for providing analogs for the intellectual realities.

In Fig. 9, each row has eight circles, yet because of the physical proximities, we tend to perceive them as groups of two (top row), groups of two and three (middle row), and groups of four (bottom row).

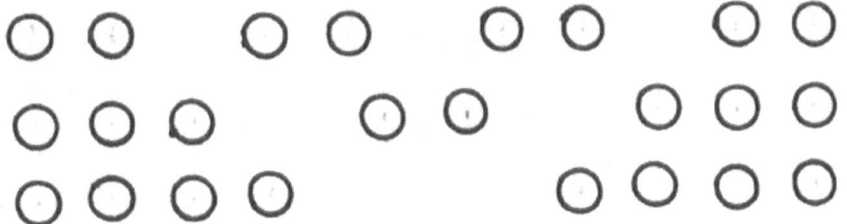

Fig. 9. Effect of grouping within equal populations

The proximity of attributes—the similarities—tends to make us consider Fig. 10 as rows of pluses or minuses rather than as similar columns of alternating symbols, even though the spaces between rows and columns are equal.

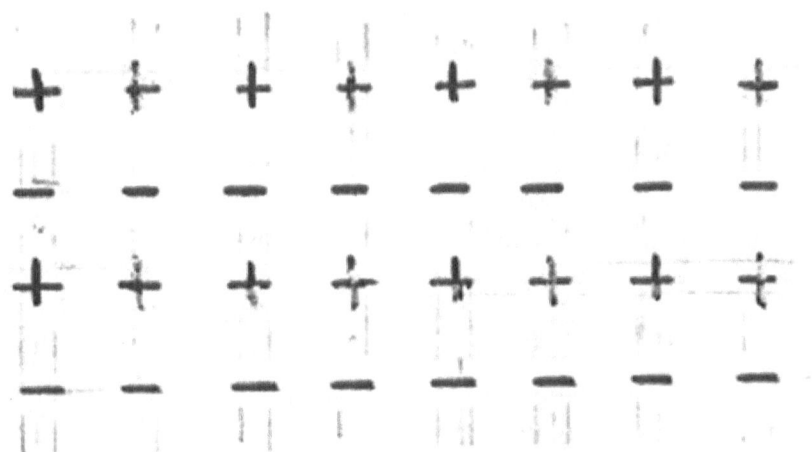

Fig. 10. Effect of similarity and dissimilarity.

Apart from visual perceptions, proximity of qualities in our intellectual perceptions can lead to simplistic evaluations. Too frequently, we will react to a situation based on only the most obvious similarities, saying, "That's exactly what happened last time," or using a cliché like, "History repeats itself." More significantly, that sort of judgment leads to remarks, such as that by former Vice President Spiro Agnew, to the effect that once you've seen one slum, you've seen them all.

When white westerners say that all blacks or Orientals look alike, such judgments become pejorative and are provocative to those in the groups. At worst, our tendency to emphasize the differences between ourselves and others, ignoring the similarities we share as well as the differences *within* each group, leads to stereotyping and prejudice. This cavalier failure to discern or to evaluate differences versus similarities is another one of those perceptual hurdles that is not only insensitive but denies us the deeper understanding we may need to cope with a situation and resolve problems by seeing a different viewpoint.

Context also is a factor in proximity. For example, a person in Buffalo, New York, may feel closer in spirit and interests to a person in Los Angeles, California, than he does to a person in Toronto, Canada, when a national concern such as defense is being considered. Yet in evaluating problems of acid rain or sharing an electric power outage in a devastating blizzard, citizens of Buffalo and those of Toronto may feel much closer to each other than to those in sunny Los Angeles.

So common purpose or common fate are part of the proximity reaction. As Benjamin Franklin said in signing the Declaration of Independence, "We must all hang together; else we shall all hang separately." Other common remarks attest to the prevalence of this kind of perception, such as, "the family must stick together through thick and thin," "in unity there is strength," and "politics makes strange bedfellows."

So do we urge members of a group to give extra effort to sustain it when its fortunes are waning? We strive to maintain the image of a group we want to protect, even though severe differences exist within it. This reflection of the human tendency toward cohesion for survival shows up even though individual members may disagree with corporate policies, an organization's viewpoint, or statements to project "national resolve." That perceived similarities may hide only a tenuous advantage is what permits opponents to divide and conquer.

Assimilation and contrast. Think of a person who comes to his office dressed in a bathing suit or a person who shows up at the beach dressed for a business meeting. Each would be considered bizarre even though the specific attire might be perfect for its normal use. Also, a bikini seen in 1950 stood out as daringly radical, but by 1980, a full-form bathing suit seemed old-fashioned. It is the way we contrast with the preponderance of perceptions or assimilate differences within a background that governs here.

Referring again to diagrams, consider Fig. 11 as an extreme case.

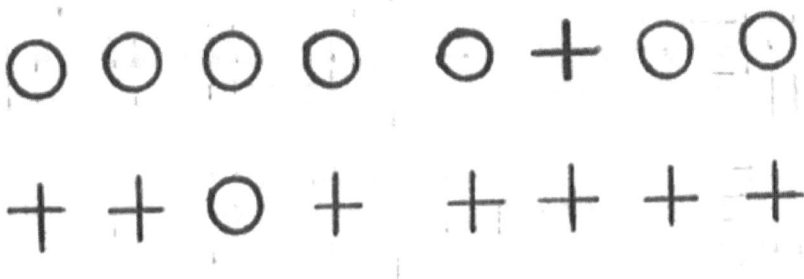

Fig.11. Effect of small differences versus large similarities.

Each group is similar in one respect in that it contains one member of the other group. Yet this shared characteristic would undoubtedly be considered too insignificant, in view of the basic differences, for members of each group to acknowledge the commonality. In ethnic or political groups, our shared attribute as humans, as residents of a particular area, as professionals, etc., may not be considered powerful enough to overcome perceived cultural or physiological differences. This is the opposite of politics making strange bedfellows.

The specific situation would determine how much weight we give to context in making our evaluation of the similarities or differences. This illustrates that we have to be aware of these contextual effects and not jump to conclusions based only on the similarities or the differences themselves.

This kind of grouping comes up frequently in evaluating how well a job has been carried out. For example, in political affairs, the in-group will always boast about how much it has done to reduce poverty (the pluses), disregarding its deficiencies in combating crime (the minuses). The out-group, putting greater emphasis on the need for crime prevention, will emphasize how much it has done in this area, downplaying their opponents' moves to reduce poverty. Or the group in power will point out how much it has already done while those out of power will accuse them of how much is yet to be done. The face/vase image of Fig.7 illustrates this half-full/half-empty controversy.

How much is enough is an eternal question. In Fig. 9, how closely together would the groups of circles need to be before we failed to think of the spaces between them as significant? Or, in Fig. 10, how far apart would the rows need to be for us to see the unity of pattern in the vertical columns?

Here again a diagram will help. In Fig. 12, if a group (at P_1) is seen to be far away from us (at P_2) on any characteristic, such as political opinion, substantive differences within that group ($P_a - P_b$) are not perceived or are minimized. That is, they are *assimilated* because both groups are at a great distance from the observer. Conversely, for groups closer to us (as at P_2), small differences ($P_c - P_d$) will be *contrasted* and maximized.

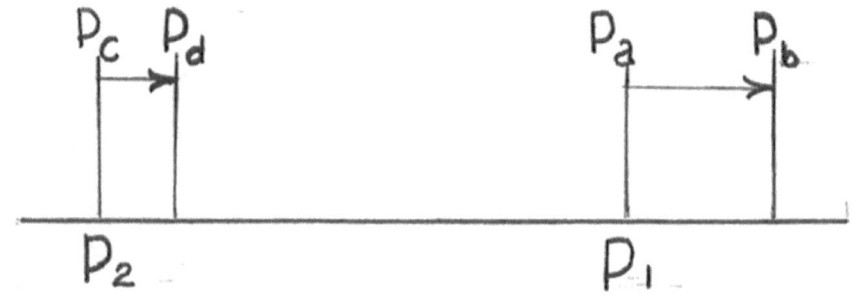

Fig. 12. Assimilation and Contrast.

Several wheels are turning in our heads at once in such matters. One has to do with perception itself—our common goal may lead us to selectively fail to see the differences in our own group. Another revolves around values—our common goal may cause us to excuse differences that we do see even though we feel they have a negative value. But as to the *degree* of difference, members of a closed group—from married couples, to country clubs, to large corporations—may see the foibles of fellow-members in sharp detail while failing to recognize significant differences in the outside group. Thus we often hear, "Why don't other people argue like we do?"

These are examples of static situations, but assimilation and contrast operate in ongoing behavior.

If a child says to a parent, or one spouse says to another, "Nothing I ever do pleases you," we have a situation similar to that diagrammed in Fig. 12. The wife at P_c, for example, accommodating her husband, moves to P_d. The contrast with her original position seems great to her, yet she claims that her new position still displeases her husband. He at P_1 views the move as a small one, for it is assimilated relative to the distance between them, which for him is still great.

This kind of thinking exists on a broad and most dangerous scale in international confrontations, such as between the US and the USSR during the Cold War. If either side tested a nuclear device, the other said, "See what warmongers they are?" Yet if one side declared a moratorium on testing, the other was apt to say, "It's only a ploy!" The US versus Iraq is another example. It is the value placed on the relative difference that makes a difference.

How can one evaluate the relative difference? Even the proportions need to be evaluated as to when they become significant. There is no mathematical rule that can be applied, but there are two psychological components that we have to be aware of. There is the substantive component that deals with the facts, and the emotional component that deals with the value or attitude we bring to those facts.

The average person sets his ratios, by and large, from a gut reaction based on built-in prejudices and mindsets, economic and pragmatic aspects, matters of convenience, and so on. He sets these ratios most likely without much thought and, even more likely, without first expressing them definitively. The proportions are apt to be fluid and arrived at unconsciously. (These are my assertions, based on personal experience.)

The "Halo Effect" and More

The subject of opinion-formation, obviously extremely broad, has attracted a lot of attention from psychologists and poll-takers. These more sophisticated evaluators have had to be more scientific, so they call on statistics (that is, calculations and not mere data) to support the way viewpoints shift and the reasons why.

The verdict is not in on how we decide upon the *degree* of contrast or assimilation, nor can it ever be in any definitive way. The situations are too complex and subjective. Understanding the dynamics and factors involved, though, should equip us to analyze such contentious matters in a more mature way.

One corollary of these perceptual dynamics is "the halo effect." In this case, we tend to let an opinion about something affect our opinion of another or related aspect of that thing in the same direction. In this way, we maintain a consistent overall view, which is comforting, but "the halo effect" is a hidden source of bias in our evaluations.

Another corollary is the echelon of evaluations that can build upon misperceptions—the "he thinks that I think that he thinks . . ." process. Let's say a person has an opinion about a friend. The friend has a view about how the first person perceives him. The first person, A, in turn, may have his own view of what his friend, B, thinks A's view of him is. In such dual evaluations, each person's view of the other's perception of him or of his opinions may be correct or not. Thus a silent duel of evaluations can continue *ad infinitum.* In extreme cases, anger, suspicion, and paranoia come into play. When A and B are groups as large as nations, these mutual misperceptions can become earthshaking.

Our ability to discern these aspects of grouped perceptions depends on our ability to analyze and synthesize. To see through the illusion of the cylinders in Fig. 6, for example, one has to be able to discern sizes and relationships between objects and background discretely. For closure, one needs to be able to put together the imagined links. These abilities undoubtedly involve some innate factors, but also are learned.

Many people are highly dependent on the surrounding clues to make sense of what they see. Others do not depend on the background "field" and tend to be more creative thinkers. The former are called "field dependent." Such people are more apt to evaluate something based on the opinion of sources whom they find credible than on their own analysis. The credibility of the source is more important than the information itself. Some reasons for this will be discussed in Chapter 11.

Selective perception will lead some people to make snap judgments about a situation as if it is an element independent of context of which they are not discerning. The opposite is an uncritical dependence on context. If one too readily assimilates some observation with an existing pattern or makes connections simplistically with a background of beliefs, one risks missing nuances that might lead to more effective evaluations.

We are guilty of this when we rationalize or base evaluations on our preconceptions.

This type of thinking operates in situations where there is a similarity in the time of occurrence of two events. We assimilate the two occurrences against the background of simultaneity. In such cases, it is easy to think that the prior event is the cause of the succeeding one, leading to the "post hoc" fallacy discussed in Chapter 3. This type of thinking is at the root of superstition. There will be more to say about this in Chapter 9.

Assimilation also occurs when we try to "make the pattern fit the mold." It is comforting if we can make facts fit preconceptions or a pet theory. Even scientists are not immune to this human impulse. They may argue long and hard about whether new observations are valid and plentiful enough to discredit a cherished theory. But if a theory that appears to describe a neat structure is demolished by new facts, the scientific mind is supposed to be trained to abandon the theory unless the new opposing facts can themselves be discredited.

Are all of these built-in tendencies described above simply normal human frailties that we cannot avoid? Do we have to put up with them? No, we don't! If we understand them, our native intelligence can overcome them. This is no different, if less obvious, than overcoming other normal tendencies that limit us from maximizing our potential.

How Does Scientific Thinking Differ?

Unwillingness to give up a pet theory is an intellectual—or an ego-driven—impulse. But how do scientists overcome the hurdles of physical perception, to which they, as mortal humans, are susceptible? There are a host of techniques to avoid these hurdles.

Selective attention should not play a part in scientific work by virtue of the scientist's motivation to engage in some experiment or procedure. Generally, any project undertaken must be based on prior research, where an ongoing need for a solution is apparent. Ideally, a scientist will have methodically considered all the known or suspected factors that must be taken into account.

In practice, *selective attention* does enter in terms of the projects an individual or organization chooses to undertake. There are always more problems than can be investigated, and the knowledge to be acquired in any field is always vastly greater than the human resources available to follow-up interesting questions. An investigator's or sponsor's frame of reference, personal ego, "hot" topics of the moment, and many other pragmatic factors govern the choices.

As to *selective perception,* a scientist can rely on instruments to "perceive" all the pertinent information. To start with, the scientist is aware of Heisenberg's caution about the effect of measuring on the thing measured. So the instrument and method chosen must be commensurate with the dimensions and nature of what is to be observed.

What the instrument "sees" depends upon its power and accuracy. The degree of discrimination and the chances of error that an instrument will produce are essential characteristics of its description. They are specified in statements of "precision and bias." So the amount of misperceptions is quantified.

Lay people ordinarily have no such guides. Facts and figures that we might use as a standard on which to base opinions may be disputable, too numerous and varied, and dependent on the source.

While instruments may be acutely more sensitive than human perception, they can mask two limitations. First, an instrument can be designed to find what the researchers are looking for. If the instrument can detect only a range of phenomena that was restricted by the designer's premises and choices, it may only yield a self-fulfilling prophecy. In practice, however, this potential mechanical source of selective perception is restricted. Many knowledgeable people play a part in such designs so that the effect of even a chief designer's biased frame of reference should be virtually nil.

The second limitation is that even though recording instruments may trace every little variation in a parameter or photograph every source of light in the heavens or every mote in a cell, the extent to which the scientist takes note of them is still a function of his level of selectivities. Many recorded blips, which would be re-examined later and found to be important, have been bypassed because of selective perception, thereby slowing a scientific development. But this is not the instrument's fault. In short, use of instruments ought to be a model, a reminder, for the acuity of our perceptions.

As to *selective memory and recall,* instruments record the observations accurately and increasingly store the information in a computer. In reverse, the computer can be programmed to retrieve every pertinent fact. As such, it is imperative of science to avoid selective memory and recall.

But lest one become smug about the independence and infallibility of hardware, one has to be aware that even here the human aspect enters. The choice of key words under which to access information, whether by a program or by incidental searching, is still a human one. However, here too the group effort involved in scientific endeavors, initially or by critiquing, minimizes the chance that some recondite bit of information will not be retrieved.

Apart from the hardware, the mode of scientific practice that stretches from meticulous recording of laboratory notes to publication of research and its critiques would obviate problems of selective memory and recall. Again, this is a matter of degree and of methodology where the scientist (possibly along with lawyers) has an advantage over the man in the street.

As to *grouping* their observations into an evaluation, do scientists have a rational way to assign similarities or designate contrasts? How do they assess relative degrees of each without being arbitrary?

It would be too mechanistic to suggest that there is a hard and fast rule or a touchstone. The scientific approach would be to look for functional aspects rather than the mere appearance of what he observes. Sometimes structure or probable origin may indicate the appropriate group assignment. The main difference between scientific grouping and that of a layman, then, is to consider the functions involved. Do the observed differences between individuals make a difference?

In truth, this is often difficult to do. Having been trained to be thorough and objective, a scientist may be lulled into a self-confident or even smug assurance that he is avoiding such human tendencies, yet he may be missing or failing to give value to important facts. The fallible human may have personal reasons, failings, or a frame of reference that prevent him from attaching significance to certain aspects with selective attention. A negative view of a particular theory or body of research or enthusiasm for one's own challenge or theory may play a part. Scientists aren't perfect!

In deciding which individuals are to be included in a group, relative proportions count. The scientific approach to quantifying relies on ratios, efficiencies, percentages, and probabilities. These all relate to factors that work in opposite directions, that is, inputs versus outputs or changes versus totalities.

As will be seen in Chapter 13 on statistics, values can be calculated where a situation is slowing down or speeding up and reaching a leveling-off point. These rates and probabilities can be determined with good reliability even for some intangibles like changes of opinion.

In the last analysis, however, after all attempts at quantification have been squeezed out of the inputs to an evaluation, human preference has the last word. Poll-takers may decide that an error of plus or minus five percent in response is tolerable. Advertisers may decide that a 2 percent response on direct-mail solicitations is adequate, and researchers in the field of persuasion may decide that a 10 percent change in answers, reflecting a particular attitude, is significant. In scientific investigations, data are evaluated against a statistical chance that they could have occurred by pure chance, but the degree of probability chosen is also somewhat arbitrary.

So there is no absolute standard for the particular number chosen in any field. All that can be said is that there is a presumably rational method that somewhat establishes a standard for evaluation and for decision-making. The bottom line when lumping observations together is to remember to ask, as the scientific mindset would, "Is this a difference that makes a difference?"

Closure motivates scientific searches. While any intelligent person has the obligation to come to conclusions and decisions that are valid, logical, ethical, and moral, it is imperative of science to develop a theory that is by way of explanation, but is primarily for prediction. Ideally, because science (hard and soft) is ultimately traceable to evidence—tangible products or documented behaviors—it trumps the normal casual ability to reach closure by its conclusions.

Summary

What we think we see is governed by our readiness to see it, our attention, and by preconceptions that affect the observations that have to be considered. In forming categories amongst individuals, one needs to ask how significant the differences are within and between groups. These are natural human limitations.

Scientists, though susceptible to these human limitations, are trained to compensate for them in forming their evaluations. This is a matter of scientific type of thinking rather than of science, as such. Hence, it applies to the training in other professions, as it should for the non-professional.

The intertwining of the physiological and the intellectual makes up only one major input to our frame of reference. The other is human language. This is unique because, unlike that of animals, it is comprised of symbols, which are arbitrary. That very fact leads to its own built-in misperceptions, as the next chapter will show.

CHAPTER 9

Language:
Seducer and Seductress

The words spill out of our mouths. For most conversations, we are not conscious of the specific words we're going to use next. They simply come. Unless we're careful about giving an answer, such as when approaching the boss, preparing a retort, or anticipating a formal speech, we mull over very little what we're going to say or how we'll say it. Psycholinguists refer to this human ability as "competence." Is it really likely that this language, which flows so freely and is under our control, can be controlling *us* to some extent?

Groping in our semantic file drawer for the right word is something we all do at some time, aware of connotation as opposed to denotation. Most people are aware of how euphemisms put a pleasant face on some unpleasant reality. We avoid death by calling it "passing away," taxes are called "revenue enhancement," and diverted funds are "laundered." We may be cynical about advertisers' use of positive-valued words (e.g., success, happiness, pleasure) to make us buy one product in preference to another, even as we succumb to them. But these are the more obvious ways that language can shape our frame of reference.

Some shaping of language has been more open and constructive. People who used to be called "colored" or "negro" defiantly turned the negative connotations of darkness—nighttime, fear, soot, etc.—into "Black is beautiful" and African-American. Another example stems from the structure of English and many other languages in the use of the masculine gender. The feminist movement of the mid-twentieth century liberated women from this linguistic bias by expunging the word "man" from sexist words and by sensitizing people to say "he or she" instead of using only the male pronoun. Comedians have examples that carry this to ridiculous extremes, but the feminist claim has awakened us to the effect on our frame of reference of the automatic use of the male noun and pronoun—the subtle, continued acceptance of a male bias in a male-dominated society. English in this sense is less sexist than other languages where the articles, adjectives, and even prepositions have to agree with the gender of the noun and where the plural of many nouns is automatically masculine.

This may all seem inconsequential, arcane, or quaint. But try to imagine the frame of reference, the conceptualization of things as having gender, that is induced in young people from the moment they begin to understand language: the automatic, unconscious acceptance of masculine dominance or preference. (This does not mean, however, that there will be no male chauvinism in a culture whose language, such as Magyar, has no grammatical forms for gender.)

Languages did not grow in a vacuum, of course. They reflect the attitudes of the cultures that use them. In millennia past, in most societies—as is still true today—women were considered to have an inferior status to men. So it is natural that languages should reflect this. One may ask, then, which is the chicken, and which is the egg? One may grant that the cultural attitudes came first and that the language developed to express them. This is exemplified in the way our language usage has changed from the influence on our culture from the "women's lib" movement and from "blacks." But as languages became established, those newly born into a language/culture were undoubtedly conditioned by the existing patterns of that language.

The feminist reaction against the predominance of the male gender in nouns and pronouns attests in a contemporary, pragmatic way to the effect of linguistic determinism. This hypothesis, formulated first by Edward Sapir in his *Language: An Introduction to the Study of Speech,* was expanded considerably by his pupil, Benjamin Lee Whorf. Originally a chemical engineer who worked for a fire insurance company, Whorf studied American Indian languages extensively.

The Sapir-Whorf hypothesis holds that language unavoidably structures the way we perceive the world. Sapir initially pointed out that the availability of words describing categories offers a "classificatory suggestiveness." Thus, when a young child scribbles a line, it may be suggested to him or her that this one is "straight," this one "curved," and that one "zig-zag." The child's future descriptions will follow this deductive pattern of classifying lines. (He may still describe a wavering line by some delightful gibberish of his own!) This is consistent with the scientist's realization that nature doesn't consist of categories or laws; we impose these names and rules on nature. Once we have named categories in our passion for order, we fit new observations into them. We refer to them as "definitions," as though they existed before the things themselves. This tendency has a subtle deductive power. We assume from the name a myriad of attributes (Danger: Stereotypes at work!). In truth, this tendency coexists with the way culture inductively changes language by adopting new words and connotations for new uses.

A few examples will illustrate Whorf's viewpoint. Arabians, famous for "Arab steeds," have no generic word for horse. For Arabs, breeding of the animal was such an intense activity that their language reflects concern with individual breeds rather than for a general class which isn't as important. (The name of a specific breed has been adopted as the generic word for "horse"). The Eskimos (the Inuit) have no single word for snow, and Laplanders have 80 words for snow. For these people, ever—present snow is such a part of their frame of reference that they need a unique word for each condition, but none is needed for the overall phenomenon.

An English-speaking child, as he learns about the winter whiteness, won't be conditioned initially by his language to perceive these variations. To him or her, snow is snow; only when the child learns to throw snowballs or to ski will he or she want to distinguish between wet snow, powdered snow, etc. Of course in English, we can describe various conditions and types of snow, but we use longer terms or phrases to describe them. It is this discrete reflection of culture in language that leads native speakers of any tongue—particularly when it is not the language normally accepted where they live—to say, "Ah, there's no language as expressive as Yiddish (or French, or . . ."). Yet all languages have the ability to express equivalent things, however circuitously.

Apart from substantive terms, there are more fundamental differences between some languages. Western languages reinforce our preoccupation with time, as our verbs have tenses. This is not true of many Amerindian languages, which are thought to reflect the greater sense of unending time as these cultures developed as opposed to our concern with immediacy and pace, demarcated history, and scheduled futures. The Hopi, for example, must denote an event as to whether it is reported, anticipated, or generalized. Also for the Hopi, objects are categorized by form rather than by color. The Navajo have no obligatory sense of time or number in verbs or nouns. For them, it's the form of an object that is to be expressed, and this determines the verb form. Nor do they separate the actors, actions, or predicates in their syntax; people merely get passively involved.

This may only be a superficial comprehension of native languages, based on their surface syntax rather than on a cultural understanding of the languages. This in itself reflects the dangers of not fully comprehending the other's frame of reference. Deeper probing shows that some Amerindian tongues include tense with the noun, as we would say "future spouse" or "ex-husband," for example.

Research done on the Sapir-Whorf hypothesis shows that there seems to be some validity to the "weak" version called "linguistic relativism." This holds that language doesn't *determine* the cultural outlook, but probably does affect it, particularly as to the ease with which ideas can be communicated. Psycholinguists still do not know whether thought, as opposed to mere perceptions, can exist without language or whether language merely expresses thought. Most probably, as the child develops, he or she matches impressions with behavior and words that are heard. By trial and error over many micro-situations, he or she discards some associations, but the most fitting survive. Thus it need not be an either/or hypothesis of which is the chicken and which is the egg, but rather one of both capabilities developing symbiotically.

English places descriptive words—adjectives—before the nouns they modify; in Latin-root languages, the reverse is generally true. Does this say anything about the unconscious attitude of those who use those languages? It has been suggested that English speakers are much more concerned with specifying the detail before stating the general, e.g., "the wonderful performance." As such, it is considered to be an inductive language, going from the specific to the general. French, where one would say "le représentation mérveilleux," going from the general to the specific, is considered to be more deductive.

This is said to be reflected in the different approaches to the legal systems of the two nations. In English law, particulars and precedents in individual cases are developed continuously, and these subsequently constitute the body of law. In France, by contrast, a more rigorously codified system exists, and specific cases are decided according to the regulations of this system.

A reflection of this may be that English involves about twice as many words as French. English is very flexible, open, constantly changing, and, hence, democratic. The French guard their three hundred thousand standard words closely and zealously, constantly warning against the bastardization by other languages. (They are not alone in that regard, however. For many nationalist groups, their language is their very soul and they resent any deprecation of it—even as they fail to acknowledge that their own language contains much borrowing from other tongues.)

By no means is this meant to denigrate French or similar languages. It merely suggests a difference in the way a French child may learn to evaluate situations as he or she grows up, compared to an English-speaking child. Learning a more deductive language with a more limited, prescribed lexicon than English conceivably may nourish a more authoritarian mindset. One may never know what aspects of an ancient culture led to peculiarities of its language. Such questions are the stuff of endless PhD dissertations.

The tie between language and attitude shows up in another contemporary context: in computer language used between the Japanese and the English. The indirect approach of the Japanese in social and business conversations is reflected in and nurtured by their language. But computer languages such as Fortran, Cobol, etc., are based on the direct approach of English expressions. In trying to express their indirect attitude in those languages, the Japanese translations become very stilted. This makes establishment of an internationally codable software more difficult for them, according to Taigu Kobayashi, the chairman of the board of Fujitsu, Ltd.[5] In addition, the Japanese try to a greater extent than is customary for speakers of English to anticipate how the reader will react to the use of a particular phraseology. Therefore, Kobayashi maintains that "human relations are unfavorably affected" by the programmed directness of English-based computer language.

The "Is of Identity"

Earlier I noted how language absorbed unconsciously in tiny increments is taken for granted as we use it. As language has grown and changed willy-nilly through the ages, many loose usages guide us ever so imperceptible into incorrect assumptions or biases. For example, we customarily say, "A rose is red," or with a trifle more exactness, "The color of the rose is red." To reflect what we know about physics and perception, languages ought not

---

[5]   "News and Trends," *Production Engineering*, Aug., 1982, p. 8

to permit the former statement. We ought to say, "The rose appears red" or "The color looks red to me."

Is this not all a fatuous circumlocution? After all, we know when we say, "The rose is red," that there is no inherent redness in the rose, but rather some pigmentation or texture that, under normal white light, absorbs all but the red wavelengths. Also, to a color-blind person, the rose might not appear red. And under fluorescent light, it might have another color. But we can't go through all these explanations. So we take it for granted that this is what we mean by the shorthand phrase.

The use of the verb "is"—in what the general semanticists call the "is of identity"—colors the relationships we perceive and the evaluations we make. When a little child is shown a picture in a nursery book, the text, teacher, or parent will say, "This is a cow." If we are more careful, we may say, "This is a picture of a cow." But so often we leave out that intermediary. We ask, "What is this?" and are delighted if the little darling answers, "That's a doggie."

Obviously, such language is a shortcut for simplicity and practicality. We hope to get children to recognize the species, rather than be concerned about the niceties of grammar. Nor do we want to introduce a sense of indefiniteness, tentativeness, or skepticism to them at this age. We expect these attitudes to come as they grow older.

The problem is that this use of language creates a tendency and then a habit of an initial, spontaneous, unthinking acceptance that the object of the sentence is, simply and totally, what the sentence says about the subject. The connection is so subtle that we are not aware of it, conditioned as we have become by the subliminal effect of our language.

It is not so terrible if a little child says, "That is a doggie" if, in fact, it shows a fox. We can correct him. But what about characteristics that are not self-evident? If a person is identified as an engineer, a writer, or a professor, we may think that the person doesn't appear or act like our image of such a description. Unless some pragmatic action hangs upon it, we don't challenge the designation or try to verify it. However, when the verb "to be" is tied to a characteristic, people may accept that description to their detriment if they depend upon a person who doesn't live up to that description.

Still more intangible, what if the characterization refers to an attribute dealing with the person's beliefs, character, or temperament? If it is said that a person is a member of some group with whose opinions we are in severe disagreement, the characterization might arouse our biases. Differences that should not make a difference may be activated, and we may take the wrong stance, often precipitously, to our disadvantage or to that of the person so identified. It is an old political trick to tarnish one's opponent by saying, "He is a Communist (or a traitor, a pervert, etc.)."

The identification need not be negatively valued, of course. We might have unwarranted feelings of self-justification and pride if we accepted flattery too easily, just as we might respond too defensively if someone told us, "You are stupid," "You are a bastard," or "You are a liar."

We assume that as we grow to adulthood we will learn to reserve judgment and not take things for granted until solid evidence is at hand. But by accepting what's tied to "is," we may be accepting as solid evidence some identification that fits our preconceptions, biases, or opinions. We slip into this pattern by imperceptible increments, making mechanistic one-to-one correspondences in a childlike way. The result? Clichés and uncritical judgments, such as, "Life is tough," "Mexicans are lazy," "Sex is dirty/great/boring," and so on.

Language itself is not the sole culprit in this immaturity, of course. However, it is hard to separate the effects of language used from the dogmatic attitudes that employ such language. The conjectured effect of this use of "is" may not have been heavily researched, but the effect can be realized if we think how easily we are satisfied by merely being told the name of something we can't identify—a bird whose call intrigues us, for example. Being told what it "is" establishes that it is recognized by someone, and that there is probably a plethora of information pertaining to it that we can research if we wish. We rest content knowing that it is not some unknown phenomenon from outer space.

Is it not a basic, innate response for us to see something, associate it with some attribute, and then join the two by simple identification? Precisely, but it is a primitive and simplistic one. It is as if by having this jewel of a tool, the naming of things satisfies our desire for certainty. It is as if by identification we can posses and control the things we name.

Similarly, labels stick and thereby seem to identify all the characteristics of a thing or person. Stereotype strikes again! This is a reaction to signs for which there are one-to-one correspondence, rather than to symbols, which are arbitrary and varied. The former is a holdover of a primitive response; the latter a more mature one. It must have taken the human race eons to develop symbolic language from signal grunts and groans, not to mention centuries to develop refinements leading to the thick and varied dictionaries of our day. In a very loose way, maturing of the individual seems to retrace that development, a process that is still occurring.

The Magic of the Word

We all share an awe of the word. Evanescent in time and sound, it can nevertheless be as lethal as a weapon. A few syllables, a few marks on a surface, a short breath, or simple stroke of the hand can dazzle. Where would we be without this tool of expression for our reasoning ability? Recognition of this can be found in the start of the Gospel according to John in the King James Version of the Bible: "In the beginning was the Word, and the Word was with God, and the Word was God."

This awe was beautifully depicted in the film *The Miracle Worker*, where Helen Keller, blind and mute since infancy, realizes that the actual liquid she touches can be represented by the symbols for "w-a-t-e-r."

That there is an atavistic response to the magic of words still shows up in language in little ways. Many people still believe in curses and hexes; it is suspected that people have become ill or have even died from the psychosomatic effects of having had such pronouncements made against them.

Even seeing a word in print can sometimes revolt us. Orthodox Jews consider that to print the word "God" blasphemes the Old Testament injunction against graven images. It was not so long ago that one would see only "d—n" in a newspaper, if you saw it at all, as if we didn't know what the dashes meant. And despite the unshackling of scatological words in books and movies, newspapers won't even print "s—t." One might say that's only avoiding unpleasant language and distasteful subjects for civility's sake. Yet even when the subject matter is appropriate, saying or printing the words is a no-no. We may smirk at these examples as reflecting hypocrisy, lack of sophistication, or modernity, yet we still knuckle under the compelling magic of the word.

That the magic of words can evoke this awe while suppressing analytical thought is seen in our responses to paradoxes. If we hear that an ancient Greek said, "All Cretans are liars, and I am a Cretan," we're left wondering as to whether he is telling the truth or not because we take the words at face value. We are wowed by what seems to be a complete, definitive statement, unaware of the unstated implication that all Cretans are liars—except the speaker.

The way the mind reacts to a word is far more complex than we may realize. With normal hearing, mental abilities, and a basic literal comprehension, this reaction occurs with near-electronic speed. But consider all that goes on: (1) We hear the sound, and then (2) we search our mental dictionary for the meaning, which may not be immediately available or clear. (3) At this point, we may reserve judgment on the meaning until the next word or words are spoken so that we can make sense of the grammar or context; (4) only then do we compare the meaning with the facts of the situation referred to. (5) We then have some kind of internal response to the meaning-in-context. (6) We formulate an external response, and 7) finally, we express that response. What a computer program that is!

But many words—or people—short-circuit this process at the second step. With the click of a neuron, we respond to the first impression and jump to the fifth step; the sound-meaning triggers emotional associations or substantive bias. Thus, if someone says to us, "You are fractious," our response may be, "What does 'fractious' mean?" If we hear, "You are too casual," we may ask the person how we ought to interpret "casual"? If we hear, "You are a liar!" our reaction would most likely be immediate disagreement or anger.

With direct characterizations, one can appreciate the arousal. Unfortunately, this response is carried over to terms that have indirect associations, that is, to abstractions. Concepts such as capitalism, communism, family virtues, national honor, and others over how the flag is waved provoke too often a response to the word (or to the flag!) as a signal. We are conditioned to react to the word as if it were the thing itself. This is especially so if the subject is dear to our heart, and still more so if it is linked by "is" to a characterization.

By allowing ourselves to be awed by the magic of words, we are led down the path to misinterpretation. We have to take the time and mental energy to stop, reflect, and probe for levels of meaning and significance.

Other Aspects

Languages have other means by which they influence how we make evaluations, e.g., simile and metaphor, dramatic or pompous words, and other rhetorical devices. Those, however, are matters of style. They are overt. They are not strictures of language structure that surreptitiously mold a person's thought. When used honestly to describe, clarify, emphasize, inform, or persuade rather than to obfuscate, they are valid.

Miscellaneous peculiarities of sentence structure were discussed in Chapter 2. Though they may not reflect or influence a frame of reference, a few reminders are in order, such as how the position of a word can affect the meaning of a sentence (as in the difference between "Everything is not hunky-dory" and "Not everything is hunky-dory"). In that respect, not all people are that careful—or all people are not that careful! Nor do we savor the subtle difference in emphasis if we place a word like *however* at the beginning, middle, or end of a sentence.

The proper use of "can" and "may" that our teachers drilled into us in elementary school are widely ignored. So are the ambiguities between obligation and anticipation inherent in "must," "should," and "supposed to be." Ambiguities in a specific word or in sentence structure were also pointed out. Undoubtedly, one's frame of reference would activate the selectivities of perception described earlier.

So the cultural inertia of the language we are born into, its sexist effects, the is-of-identity, the magic of words, and word placement all show that language can indeed be a seducer and seductress of the inputs to our evaluations.

How Scientists Avoid the Seduction

In general, the scientist's approach to the use of language is one of precision, economy of word usage, avoidance of dramatic words in favor of objective ones, and standardized definitions and descriptions. Also, in the organization of reports, fact is kept separate from opinion—the scientist's personal, subjective opinions are customarily noted in a separate "Discussion" section, in which the writer has free reign to say what he or she will about what has been observed.

Precision can be seen at its acme in mathematics, the most abstract of languages. As was seen in Chapter 2, various conventions for stating numbers with decimal precision are used. Even the uncertainty of a number can be made definitive by stating the tolerances, the limiting values for a formula, or the approaches of a function to some value.

Words don't have those luxuries, but scientific language has its refinements. Even standard definitions aren't standard for all time. There is always an ongoing review of definitions by scientific organizations as demanded by new information rather than by casual usage. Because definitions are based on function or appearance that can be rigorously measured, connotations are avoided.

Perhaps the paragon of a functional statement was posed succinctly by Shakespeare when Romeo asked, "What's in a name?" He gives with eternal charm the answer that the modern scientist would say is a functional one. But scientific speech is thought of as flat, dry, and dull, not Shakespearean. So what does a scientific approach to language have to offer the ordinary person?

First of all, we are not talking about casual, social conversation in this frame of reference. We are concerned with language used for some significant purpose. That is where the scientific approach is a suitable model.

To match that approach, the layperson has to have an adequate vocabulary. Just as the scientific mindset constantly probes one level deeper to any answer given, so language over time has broken down general words to give us still more specific subdivisions to express nuances of meaning. An ample vocabulary is an arsenal of weapons to target specific factors for making evaluations. The word is our servant not our authoritarian master to seduce us into incorrect deductions. This aim for scalpel-like precision obviates the magic effect of a word.

Another example to follow is to try to keep opinion separate from observation. Note: I say "observation," not "fact." It's all too easy for many of us to fail to distinguish one from the other. We have to constantly remember that evidence is the premise for scientific discourse. Our evaluations and the way we communicate them ought not to be impulsive, arbitrary, or based on unexamined impressions that what we see is actually fact. Objectivity is the watchword here.

Acknowledging the perceptive risks of observations and keeping them separate from fact allows one to avoid the "is of identity." If someone says, "This is a clear case of mental fatigue," there is an implied assumption that other knowledgeable scientists would agree. For those who might disagree, discussion would cover the subjective factors. Instead of saying what "is," the scientific mode might say "This appears to me to have the characteristics of . . ." Long-winded, too guarded, too indefinite? Perhaps.

But consistent with the scientists' attitude of tentativeness, relativism, and indeterminacy, it defuses impulsivity and dogmatism.

Summary

This chapter has touched on some cultural and structural aspects of language that can affect our frame of reference and the evaluations we make in very subtle ways. They are pitfalls that go hand in hand with our perceptual filters and with the concept of the measurer affecting the thing measured by virtue of the tools used.

Since language has to be used to think about and communicate whatever we do, many thinkers feel that linguistic lenses contribute to the parallax of our own substantive frame of reference. More deeply seated inputs will be the subject of the next chapters.

PART III

THE FOUR AS

CHAPTER 10

Aristotle:
Genius and Nemesis

Time for a break. Two major stones for building the foundation of evaluations are now in place. One is our mode of perception, with its all-too-human limitations, and the other is our tool of language, which can influence us in subtle ways even as we use it. Building on these two stones, we tend to generalize too broadly, define things too loosely, and identify things, people and situations with attributes too carelessly.

Together these add to a pattern in communication that has existed through the ages. As far back as ancient Greece, Aristotle wrestled with the eternal problems of understanding reality and expressing it meaningfully. The old philosopher had a voracious curiosity and pursued a vast range of interests methodically. Although he was wrong about a great number of things, as one might expect from the primitive technology of his time, his influence in the area of communications and logic persist to this day. So it is worthwhile to spend a little time telling a bit about the old guy.

Two big problems of his time (about 400 BCE) absorbed Aristotle. The first problem was understanding reality, which involved names, definitions, and relationships of things. The second problem involved the statements made about them.

As to the first, philosophers, observing how things changed (e.g., an apple grew from a seed to ripeness, and then rotted), wondered what the permanent essence must be. A rotting apple appeared different in many respects from a ripe one, yet it was still an apple. Was there some "apple-ness" inherent in it? Did change come about because of an inherent "rottingness"?

Plato, who was Aristotle's teacher, believed that there were "ideas" or "ideals"—somewhere out there in the blue—that represented the real essence of a thing. Aristotle felt that this essence was in "forms," inherent in the thing itself. The difference between teacher and pupil did not matter. What mattered for practical reasons and for establishing the truth about reality was how you identified a thing so as to be sure you were defining that particular thing. The word had to represent only that thing; the name for a group of things would have to avoid subjective characterizations for individual differences; and one would have to find the least common denominator for similar things that deserved to be represented by that name. With that established, reasoning would be the tool (in the absence of scientific ones) to explain the reality.

To do this in an orderly way, Aristotle established his "Laws of Thought," codifying his observations as to how people think. The first law, the Law of Identity, stated that a thing could only be what it is. This might seem fatuously self-evident, but it was a standard, a base to start from. This could be represented by A = A. To make this more rigorous, the second law, that of Contradiction, said that a thing can be either A or not A. As if that were not enough, the third law, that of the Excluded Middle, wraps things up by proclaiming that a thing can be either A or B, but not both.

Such circumlocutions may seem labored and superfluous in our day, but such was the great perplexity about the nature of things that Aristotle aimed, in effect, to give 'em a right, give 'em a left, and then give 'em both together to pin down an entity.

Apart from naming and identifying, however, there was the ultimate motivation of seeking not merely knowledge but truth. This was the philosophical driving force behind the argumentation used by Socrates as described in the dialogues by his pupil Plato, who, in turn, taught Aristotle. That motivation could have stood on its own two feet, but there was another reason why it was so necessary in those days to know the truth of a situation: It was a practical and historical matter.

Disruptions from the Persian and Peloponnesian Wars had led to many legal problems, so a cadre of people arose who could argue cases in the courts. Most of the population, after all, was uneducated and needed such representation. In time, as might be expected, legal "ambulance chasers," wordsmiths who would sell their verbal skills despite the absence of wisdom, became prevalent. A trend of arguing fine points for their own sake developed. This style of clever, if not necessarily valid reasoning we now call "sophistry," though the term discredits the original Sophist philosophers. They had argued that objective truth could never be discovered. Socrates argued against this, engaging people in discussions of issues by his method of dialectics. He would challenge his hearer's arguments by drawing out their implications and posing the opposite viewpoint. Though his aim was to try to reach the truth through dialogue, he never resolved any questions. Persuading people of the truth through valid reasoning rather than through sophistry or diffuse argumentation became a pragmatic as well as a philosophic necessity. Someone had to try to bring order out of this chaos. That someone was Aristotle.

The rigor of his approach was actually consistent with what we now consider to be a scientific one, for he was aiming for definitions that were precise, unambiguous, and unique as standards for logical argument. These definitions could transcend changes of condition or appearance and would avoid differing subjective opinions. Thus, if two situations, A and B, shared certain attributes for the sake of logical argumentation, only those shared attributes could be considered as belonging to A and B (see Fig. 13).

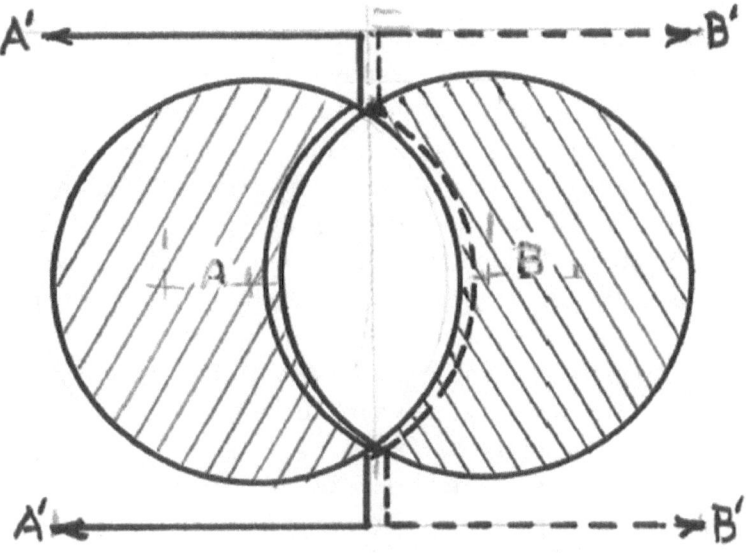

Fig. 13. Schematic illustration of situations (A and B) sharing some of the same attributes. For purposes of logical argumentation, only the unshared aspects, A' and B', are considered as representing or defining the respective situations.

Aristotle could start only with existing words, though. He believed that you could get to the truth of things through the statements that were made about them.

Sad to say, however orderly this usage was, it didn't actually explain causes or reality as we know science can do today. Definitions were merely verbal surrogates for a thing, seemingly providing comprehension and finality, yet really empty of intrinsic meaning. Lost in the effort was a realization that the habit of looking at the world in this way leads to a simplistic and dogmatic mindset in the unsophisticated. Nuances and implications tend to be ignored. A one-to-one identity of a thing with its attributes develops, as does a tendency to either/or evaluation. Nevertheless, it was a good try by the old genius.

Establishing identities through words was not enough for the great philosopher. Orderliness—establishing relationships between things—was a logical extension of identities. How could one relate one thing to another in some rational way in the statements we made? Aristotle's unique contribution in this regard was to systematize reasoning by developing the syllogism. This mode of figuring out how one thing related to another through their mutual attributes is firmly with us today.

In its most well-known and simplest form, the syllogism consists of three statements. The first statement, or major premise, gives a generalized statement, tying together a large category (a person, thing, or situation) with an attribute. The second statement, or minor premise, refers to a particular member of that group in the major premise. The third and final statement is a conclusion that says the smaller category (e.g., the species) must necessarily share the attribute(s) of the larger one (e.g., the genus) of the major premise. So, one might say that if all As have X, and B is a member of Group A, B must also have attribute X. The deduction is as mechanical as the meshing of two gears.

Aristotle developed many forms of the syllogism—with didactic brilliance, if in boring detail—to cover all sorts of contingencies. For example, if some As have X, and C is a member of A, does C necessarily have X? Or, if A does not have X, and C is a member of A, can C have trait X?

In common conversation, we might hear someone say, "That's an interesting deduction," when what they really mean is that only an opinion has been expressed. A true deduction has an arithmetic meaning: a subtraction from a larger group or a drawing down. It is the opposite of induction, used in scientific method, whereby the specific case has to be given first and in multiples so that the conclusions can be summarized from their common elements. Induction goes upward from species to genus.

The syllogism lends itself readily to simplified instruction, but it has inherent problems. What if the major premise is wrong or purely subjective? A good illustration of this is that famous paradox of Epimenedes that says, "All Cretans are liars; I am a Cretan; therefore I am a liar." If you play around with this, you can see that if the major and minor premises are true, the conclusion cannot be; that is, having made the first two claims, even the conclusion could be a lie. Yet we are so wowed by the magic of words, so ready to believe the statement proffered by an authoritative person, that we accept the major and minor premises as gospel.

A similar problem with this pattern of reasoning is that it is circular in getting to the truth of the major premise. Consider this classic: "All men are mortal; Socrates is a man; therefore Socrates is mortal." Well, if Socrates is mortal, he's not alone—so is every other person. That all adds up to inductive evidence for the first statement. That's okay *if* the observation that contributes to it does not have built-in biases or misstatements. A huge problem with the way we make evaluations is that people too often start with major premises that reflect summations of knee-jerk or incorrect responses to their observations. This is-of-identity reinforces a transformation; the thing becomes the same as its characterization, even though "the map is not the territory." Despite an understandable tendency to make such links where they commonly exist, the scientific mind has to keep them scrupulously separate. In examining new examples of a group, one ought to say, "Hold on! Even though this C is part of A, it might not share all of A's Xs." Statistical verification would be needed. Apart from these quantitative variations—how many Cs are part of A—it is very difficult to cover qualitative ones. That is, does C have more or less of a certain characteristic?

Let's face it: Most of us are not about to clutter up our assertions with "in 98.44% of cases . . ." Most people don't study Aristotle, nor do they have to succumb to the lure of the syllogism. There is a normal, psychological desire to believe something clean, neat, and positive. The effectiveness of the syllogism over the ages has been that it is prescriptive. It begins and continues with telling you how things are and winds up telling you how a particular case must be. This is the way children are taught in the most general terms. It is the easiest, most practical, most authoritative style for parent or teacher. There is something commonsensical and intuitive about it. These facts alone would have kept it as a mode of reasoning for millennia, but apart from these practical reasons, there are historical reasons, too.

After Aristotle died in 322 BC, his teachings gradually died out and eventually his works were thought to be lost.[6] They languished only in the words of various translators. Approximately a millennium later, some of his works were found in the basement of a ruined building. So in the sixth century, with the original Greek available, these works (mainly those dealing with logic) were translated into Latin by Boethius. This man, one of the last students at Plato's still-existent academy before it ws closed by Justinian in 529 AD, had a passion to rescue Aristotle's writings from their mistranslations. Rome had fallen by then, and scholarship began to diffuse into the Near East. The newly available, accurate translations from the original Greek works began to be translated into Arabic and Hebrew. So the great philosopher's teachings began to spread through Europe and the Near East. Gradually, the comprehensiveness, rigor, and reasonableness of Aristotle's thinking captivated the minds of thinkers.

Because the Catholic church was the major unifying power throughout Europe after Constantine's conversion to Christianity, it also was the teaching establishment of the times. Aristotle's works were venerated by the churchmen, the Scholastics, of the medieval period—though not without some early opposition within the church. Yet these writings carried the excitement of buried treasure, so Aristotle became the rage of that day. Schools were established by the church to teach the philosopher's "universals" (hence, the Universities of Paris, Oxford, and elsewhere). Rhetoric (the art of persuasion) and logic became two subjects that a person had to study to be considered educated.

The power and influence of the church was such as to make its educators authoritative. It must be said, too, that the style of thinking that was used was dogmatic and authoritarian. This had a downside. Teaching deductively, whereby one has to accept a major premise that leads inevitably to a conclusion, has had a stifling influence on independent thought, at

---

[6] His *Poetics* was discovered during the Renaissance, but his *Constitution of Athens* was not discovered until 1890 in Egypt.

least on the part of most of the population that was subjected to this style. That is not to say that there were not great thinkers within the church and through the ages. But to the extent that the premises and mode of thinking were constrained within a given frame of reference, this mode of reasoning was severely limited.

This does not mean that all deductive reasoning is invalid. But if used by people with an axe to grind or with outdated beliefs, it can become opinionated and misleading. The syllogism is useful *if* one keeps in mind the limitations of the generalizations used. The scientific approach, therefore, would apply it this way: "In X percent of cases, Y percent of the time, Class A has Z percent of these characteristics "(major premise); item from Class B appears to be a specific example of Class A with a certain statistical probability (minor premise); therefore we can conclude temporarily that Class B will share the characteristics of Class A."

That's a lot of ifs, ands, and buts, but it all builds on the information collected inductively so as to establish the major premise and leaves the future open to more inductive evidence to affirm the conclusion. This is what stimulates and allows for creative thinking. Indeed, the winds of change have been blowing in this direction since Aristotle's times.

The ferment in new thinking that came with the Renaissance and the excitement of new horizons of knowledge that came with the Age of Exploration all contributed to a rise of inductive thinking as a powerful new force. It was also a democratizing force. The way people sized up the world—making their evaluations—at least in the Western world as a whole, was becoming more sophisticated. It seemed to parallel the way we develop as individuals (as the child psychologist, Jean Piaget, has shown). The Dark Ages were similar to our infancy when we were totally dependent upon our parents or caretakers and were just awakening to the whirl of the complex, varied, undifferentiated and unstructured things around us,. We didn't know why things happened and tended to ascribe them to fantasies and fears equivalent to the animistic belief in various gods that preceded the official adoption of Christianity. The Renaissance seemed to parallel the stage of little children who have seemingly infinite curiosity; we marvel at the way kids tie what they observe with the words they hear to form simple opinions and make simple judgments in keeping with their status and environment. Yet still at that stage, we tend to believe what we are told. Gradually, as with the age of exploration, we observed variations of things we thought were fixed and learned that there are pluses and minuses to amounts, qualities, and values. Then, the Enlightenment and the Industrial Revolution were similar to our adolescence when we advance from incredulity into more independent thinking, more mature evaluations, and opinion forming. The rise of inductive thinking with the Industrial Revolution and the start of the scientific age seems to parallel this stage within our society.

Of course, in any era, some people are ahead of the curve. Stages overlap and are loosely defined. But overall, the centuries of mainly deductive thinking and teaching has shown a lot of inertia, a legacy that still survives.

It was in opposition to this long-standing, essentially autocratic mode that Alfred Korzybski in 1941 enunciated "general semantics" as a non-Aristotelian system, a designation that the Institute of General Semantics forthrightly proclaims. The "allness" of syllogistic reasoning, its mechanistic identifying of things with characteristics so conducive to stereotyping, were shown to work opposite from a scientific approach. Many psychologists and philosophers since Korzybsky have elaborated on this theme.

Now, from Aristotle, it's time to move on to the next A, authoritarianism, which picks up the thread (a rope, really) of the attitude that is implicit in teaching with the syllogism and that has pervaded so much of the teaching style of the past.

CHAPTER 11

Authoritarianism: Yours Not to Question Why

I t's not really fair to dump onto Aristotle all the blame for the legacy of deductive thinking, as it was nurtured by other forces acting together, I'd say.

One of these forces was the natural style of parenting, as mentioned earlier. For parents to tell their children what to do, what not to do, and, above all, to obey, is the easiest, most practical way to raise kids, if not the wisest psychologically. However, many parents through the ages no doubt used creative and inspirational ploys to motivate their children at various times and in different situations.

Another force through the ages was the existence of a monarch who set the authoritarian pattern. His (or her) rule was absolute; after all, it was said to be divinely inspired! This understanding existed on the part of the anointed leaders of society, the nobility, the lesser authorities, the Pope, and the clergy. Their authority was largely unquestioned and was most likely not recognized as authoritarian. Subservience by the slave, the serf, and the peasant was the rule. It was a case of, "Yours not to reason why, yours but to do and die." This attitude on the part of the leaders and the followers in society persisted until monarchies began to fall at the time of the First World War. Prior to that, as late as the Victorian era, the social and cultural pattern was that "children should be seen and not heard." Many of us today are still only a generation or two away from that period, and its patterns die hard.

And there's more. Part of the age-old pattern was (and still is) that the man of the house was the boss. Mama may have ruled the roost in many respects, but the cultural myth has been that the father's role was to be emulated. Certainly this was true in terms of skills of craftsmanship. "Like father, like son" and "If it's good enough for my father, it's good enough for me" were the popular slogans. These attitudes were not without merit in terms of preserving family order and much-needed physical skills. As to mental skills, however, there were some stifling effects.

In their harshest forms, these levels of authority became authoritarian. Status, which the ordinary person could accept with a fairly benign attitude, begat a malignant attitude—malignant in its effects on independent thinking styles because it was so insidious. Not until after the Second World War was the psychological damage of this style analyzed systematically and explained. The Nazis and the Fascists had been defeated. In a worldwide sigh of relief, people ruminated about how the Nazi horror and the Holocaust had come about. How could it have occurred in a nation that had contributed so much to culture in earlier centuries? A huge investigation into that question, undertaken by the American Jewish Committee, resulted in *The Authoritarian Personality* by Theodore Adorno, et al., where the authors examined the backgrounds of people who had been at the far right of the political spectrum. In a following work, *The Open and Closed Mind* by Milton Rokeach, the author recognized that the totalitarian mindset existed also at the far left side of the political spectrum.

What showed up at the end of each political view was an attitude of authoritarianism, a style so pervasive, so ordinary, that no one recognized or considered it, certainly not compared to those major and more apparent economic and political causes for the rise of totalitarian regimes. Yet it was a silent illness, affecting the attitudes and behavior of millions of people.

The way authoritarianism works is complex yet easy to understand. It goes deeper than the remarks made above about the way parents bring up their children; rather, it involves the extent and manner to which parents exert their authority. It is a style where parents insist that their children do things only when and as the parents wish at all times and to not dispute what the parents say, think, or do. In short, the kids' opinions and evaluations must replicate those of their parents. Children from such households fail to develop their own capabilities. They have no outlet to find answers by their own initiative, and their curiosity is squelched. "Curiosity killed the cat," we often tell them, when they incessantly ask "Why?" Since they are not allowed to think for themselves, the young people fail to develop their intellectual resources in terms of reaching their own conclusions. They grow to adulthood requiring the direction of others as a goad and as a guide in making decisions. Accepting direction from the top becomes the comfortable way to react, and this domineering style is transferred to those who are below them. The same is true for obedience. So hierarchy gets taken for granted. Even one's peers may be slotted into superior and inferior. People get sized up as good guys or bad guys, and this polarization is applied to life situations.

There's still more! Another psychological trait is thought to develop as a result of this autocratic upbringing. The children held back against their normal, healthy, life-challenging instincts resent not only the restraints their parents impose, but unconsciously resent the parents themselves for imposing them. Kids understand, however, that they're supposed to "honor thy father and thy mother." Indeed, kids have a normal dependence on their parents and love them, so they develop an unconscious sense of guilt about their feelings of resentment. How to expiate this? Any expression of rebellion against the parents would be met by harsh discipline and punishment. If you can't take it out on your parents, take it out on someone else. Be as harsh on them as you'd like to be against your elders, or as they might be to you. In other words, scapegoat those who seem inferior to you. Scapegoating leads to prejudice and hatred against those who are not like you. Suspicion of those who are seen as potential threats or persecutors leads to rampant paranoia. And how do you resolve these problems? By attaching yourself to some respected in-group and its icons, which gives you a sense of security. In America, the Ku Klux Klan is a prime example.

As an adult brought up in an authoritarian system, there is a mixture of attitudes: A deficient ability to form evaluations independent of authority; dependence upon and respect—even awe—for anyone in a high position of authority, with sanctioned obedience; and resentment toward those higher-ups. At the same time, a polarization in categorizing people and situations, and a discomfort with "otherness" that can become a potentially visceral hatred of people different from oneself, or xenophobia, which is then added to the lack of self-esteem and self-confidence, for you can't trust others if you can't trust yourself.

With the imaginativeness and flexibility that the child failed to develop now squelched, life is viewed as being in fixed molds with simple verities. A desire for "the good old days" leads to conservatism and a fear of progress. Situations, like people, are judged as starkly good or bad; actions to be taken have an all-or-nothing, black-or-white character.

There is still another facet of reasoning skills that come from this authoritarianism. Because of the dependence upon authority, the student tends to put complete faith in the source of information and doesn't adopt a questioning approach to the information itself. Certainly we all value the source of information, but for those people whom I am describing, the source dare not be challenged. So one-sided interpretations, selective facts, and even misinformation can get locked in. This is why many religious people believe literally in the Bible, the Koran, or other such texts, even though their selective interpretations can lead to strife between their adherents. It is this mindset rather than specific issues that fuels the conflicts between the Irish Protestants and Catholics, between the Muslims and Hindus, between the Israeli Jews and Palestinians, and between so many other ethnic and religious groups.

The thinking and learning styles of people who are so hidebound fall into two basic types, as described by Rokeach and others. One involves an inability to analyze information, which is called rigidity. The other involves a difficulty to synthesize or accept new information and is referred to as dogmatism. People with these traits cannot see the forest for the trees. These limitations are two sides of the same coin. Folks with these attributes are apt to jump from unwarranted assumptions to foregone conclusions and do not have any tolerance for ambiguity or uncertainty; a thing must be one or another, as with Aristotle's laws. Nuances or possible interpretations are missed. Relativism is anathema. "Allness" and black-or-white are the prime ways to form an evaluation. Ironically, this cognitive style is present even within people who have high degrees of formal education.

What is heard is the desire for simplicity and definitiveness, and the veneration of sources allows demagogues to thrive. Appeals to emotion, offering outlets for frustration, evoke knee-jerk reactions. Any tendency to analyze or challenge what is put forth and the willingness to consider and accept contrary views is suppressed. All the selectivities of perception come into play, as does one's inability to see their own—or the other's—frame of reference.

Undoubtedly, most people are aware of extremist groups and abhor them or think of them as nuts. What most people do not recognize, however, are the attitudes or authoritarianism that exist to one degree or another in their upbringing and what they impose upon their children.

Bear in mind that what has been presented above is a generalized model and is not the only model to describe personality. It is not an all-or-nothing case. One can be more or less authoritarian at different times or in different circumstances, and parents can still show love and other positive attributes toward their children and others at the same time. The extent of the harmful effects of authoritarianism depends upon how harshly this attitude is conveyed, how often, at what times, and in what circumstances.

How Scientists Do This

The scientific mode of forming evaluations is the antithesis of authoritarianism. Unfortunately, individual scientists may be rigid or dogmatic in their personal lives, even in holding to certain scientific concepts. But in doing so, they fail to uphold a true scientific approach. For the latter, analysis and synthesis is basic. So is awareness of the possibly tentative nature of results and of as-yet-undiscovered variations. For scientists, uncertainty is a challenge, not a thing to be feared.

Scientists do, of course, develop proof that is irrefutable for some things that we are expected to accept, but in that respect they are simply *authoritative,* providing expertise, not making a demand. At that, the true scientist has in the back of his mind the understanding that what has been "proven" at one time may still be challenged and upset at some future time.

Scientists also enunciate concepts to encompass obvious phenomena (e.g., electromagnetism or gravity). These may not be open to challenge; they are held as absolutes. How do we draw the line between some dogma offered in an authoritarian way and some accepted wisdom proclaimed by scientists? The next chapter will look into two other aspects that shed light on an answer to that question.

CHAPTER 12

Abstractions and Absolutes

So far, the discussion in this book has gone from the outputs of communication—the aspects that are apparent, like being specific, generalizing, and thinking about our frame of reference—to the inputs—those less obvious aspects, such as the effects of our selectivities, our native language, patterns of reasoning, and the probable effect of the attitudes that can limit those reasoning skills. I likened the outputs to the structure of an edifice and the inputs to its foundation. Now we come down to the bedrock of the whole enterprise.

Chapter 10 showed that the deductive style of reasoning that depends upon the syllogism is based upon a general assertion that is to be accepted as a fact and used as the basis for specific conclusions. When this prescriptive and implicitly dogmatic way of stating a premise is enforced with an authoritarian discipline, the topic presented can get locked into one's consciousness without examination. The real trouble starts when those topics deal with intangibles, that is, with concepts. These may be umbrella terms to cover valid, practical realities, but they are abstractions, meaning that they are not definitively measurable. They have a diffuse, airy quality, but they still guide our opinion formation.

But this is only the tip of the iceberg. For many of us, certain concepts have been ingrained since childhood. The process is subliminal at first, as concepts aren't introduced directly, but as attitudes and beliefs. As we grow older, they may be presented more directly. Attitudes affect our behavior, but beliefs are what motivate us and what we rely upon. What's more, they involve our values. Mess around with those, and you're in real trouble because values are intertwined with our whole being. An unexamined abstract concept triggers these values, e.g., obedience, independence, or competitiveness, and each can become an article of faith so powerful as to take on a life of its own. We instinctively fail to keep in mind what each value implies in terms of operational realities. The map again becomes the territory; the word becomes the thing it's meant to represent.

A look at the diagram of the structural differential in Chapter 3 shows how far apart the abstraction is from the reality and even the verbal level. This diagram points out a difference between abstracting and the abstraction. When a person uses a syllogism, he or she is both using an abstraction and abstracting. The major premise may be an abstraction from which the conclusion is drawn by abstracting it as a particular case. Starting with the abstraction leads to deductive reasoning, but that very abstraction, that concept, that general case, comes from inductively abstracting similar characteristics from several cases. Going upward or downward can lead to trouble if it isn't done with discernment. Either way, one's frame of reference, attitudes, beliefs, and values can skew the process.

When someone characterizes a government-sponsored health plan as "socialism," gun control as "privacy invasion," or abortion as "sin" or "individual freedom," that person is abstracting certain pragmatic aspects of these situations to classify them under a more generalized concept, an abstraction, which becomes the starting point for evaluation. Because it is value loaded, the pragmatic, nitty-gritty aspects of the issue are given no weight. Furthermore, as the starting point, the concept takes on the quality of an absolute.

The trouble is that there can be conflicting abstractions. Take gun control. This implies that a person wanting a gun cannot just go out and buy one but is required to get a permit; that is, he or she has to yield to some governmental authority within which one has only a very indirect voice. Also, one has to pay for the permit, wait until it is issued, wait to receive the gun, and register and re-register the gun periodically—a piling up of irritating infringements upon one's time and money. So it is easy to see how the eager gun buyer will build his annoyance into an abstraction of "freedom infringement." However, is there not another way to evaluate these requirements? What about safety or responsibility to oneself and the community? These, too, can be considered abstractions that have absolute value and practical consequences.

The reason one person dotes on his freedom and another is more concerned about safety has to do with one's belief system, which is the bedrock of this dynamic.

The Belief Hierarchy

Believe it or not, our beliefs are not a bunch of ideas floating around loosely in our heads. Rokeach has put them into a hierarchy where some beliefs are more potent than others. The hierarchy lends itself to sublevels. At the lowest level (I) are our unshakable beliefs, such as, the sun will rise tomorrow, we are alive, and so on. At level II are beliefs that are inculcated in us very early in our lives about how we see ourselves. Do we put ourselves down, or do we think of ourselves as movers and shakers? In short, our self-esteem and ego-strength, Level III beliefs have to do with our relationships with others, our honesty, and the way we think others see us. Level IV involves beliefs we absorb from authority figures: parents, teachers, clergy, and government, which are more specific and overt. Finally, Level V concerns the day-to-day beliefs that involve temporary events or activities like whether or not we'll go to the movies or play golf, or our interpretations from reading the news. The higher the level, the easier it is to change the beliefs and the values that we give to them.

All of these levels may be in play at the same time to a greater or lesser degree and make up a system. Level I is so basic that we don't even consider it, while Level V is so superficial that the values associated with it can be overlooked easily in most cases. The levels where problems are hidden are, in decreasing effect, II (our personas), III (relationships with others), and IV (specific beliefs absorbed from authority).

What good is this information about belief levels? What does it have to do with how we form evaluations? The answer is that it gives us insight into fundamental psychological factors that govern how we accept and use information. Such insight can only help the way we evaluate. More pragmatically, it gives us a ladder from which to examine what drives our opinions, one rung at a time, in discussing issues where tensions can arise between people.

Actually, we now have two such ladders. The first is the Structural Differential. We can match the two, rung for rung. Suppose we're in a discussion with someone about their opinions, or suppose we are simply judging opinions in the media. Better yet, what if we were honestly and analytically examining our own opinions? The ultimate outcome for doing so is expressed by the action that the opinion implies at the reality level. Unraveling the abstract idea to find this level is one way to come to more rational opinions. Unraveling the associated beliefs at each level can deepen our understanding of how those opinions were formed.

Perhaps the following table will make this a little clearer.

Abstraction	Overt Beliefs and Actions as to:	Covert Belief Levels and Values
Higher	Individual liberty	II—Self esteem, persona
Concepts	Invasion of privacy	II—Ego-strength III—Self-image, values about relationships with others
	Gov't regulations about gun control	IV—Beliefs absorbed from authority figures
Lower: Verbal level Reality level	Gun ownership & use: Obtaining permit, paying fees, etc.	V—Superficial beliefs as to required procedures

The implications of this chart are that it is not enough to think about what the specific abstraction level involves (e.g., government regulation). One should examine the belief level involved, on this point, self-image and values about relationships with others. This would then involve the rights of the gun owner and of society in general. Let's take another hot issue, abortion, for possible further clarification. The two comparisons here might be as follows:

At the highest abstraction level would be the two rights: the right of women to choose what to do with their own bodies and function versus the fetus' right to life. Each of these would involve Belief in Levels II and III—how one views oneself as well as values about life as such. At a lower abstraction level, the verbal level, the abortion proponents would call the procedure a natural medical operation, involving scheduling, costs, or location, for example. These should be balanced against other pragmatic aspects, such as the safety of professional treatment versus the harmful consequences of the inevitable "back alley" abortions if abortion were made illegal. The right-to-life proponents would call abortion a sin. That abstraction level could be equivalent to Belief Level IV, or possibly V. Terminology would have to be examined; "right to life," used to imply the life of the fetus, must also imply the right to the mother's life, physically or psychologically. From the standpoint of trying to carry on a rational discussion, it would seem illogical to pit a right (the highest abstraction) against a procedure (at the reality level). That would lead to muddled thinking. One right should be compared with another at the equivalent belief level.

There's a new problem here—calling something a sin is not simply a semantic matter, as it, too, reflects beliefs at levels II, III, and IV. Also, the reality level of a medical procedure could be subsumed under "social problem," or "psychological problem" as well as a "moral problem." Trying to fathom which belief levels are operating gets complicated.

An even tougher nut to crack is how one comes to hold certain views at that belief level. So many of our beliefs were subtly developed as we grew up, absorbed from experience, education, and inculcated by our upbringing. As mentioned earlier, the higher the belief level, the values are less potent, and the beliefs are more specific and easy to change.

It is counterproductive to try to be a psychoanalyst. So again, I ask, is there any point to this exercise? Have we not met an impenetrable roadblock? We can't expect to change one's deeply absorbed, fundamental beliefs, can we? Perhaps not, but I think it is worth trying to fathom what those underlying beliefs are when examining opinions and to decipher where those motivations come from. Arguing facts at the most superficial Belief Level (V) would get us nowhere; it could go on endlessly. But examining our deepest motivations might be fruitful for our own self-understanding and for that of others with whom we are discussing evaluations.

It is not my purpose to discuss gun control, abortion, or any other contentious issue. Apart from the issues, though, there's an indirect value to this kind of rumination. The greater our understanding of motivations, the greater our ability to target the real source of opinions that we may want to understand or try to change. If, for example, we feel that people hold some opinions because of ignorance of facts (Level IV) or from selective perception or bias (Level III), we are in a better position to try to correct those shortcomings. If we felt that an opinion was possibly tied to one's self-image or from a need to compensate for some frustration in their lives (Level II), might it not be possible to fulfill that need by alternative opinions?

Even if we don't play psychoanalyst, the point can't be made too strongly that we can get into real trouble if we don't keep our abstractions in check. If they take on the aura of an Absolute Truth, they become the thing itself and fall under no higher abstraction. If we fail to climb down the ladder to the reality levels involved, we can easily get conned. Wars have been fought because people got fired up about "patriotism," "destiny," and other high-sounding principles. No doubt we can all agree that "morality" is a top-notch abstraction. But then, who agrees on what is moral?

The difference between being motivated by high ideals doggedly pursued and being galvanized by an unanalyzed faith in an empty concept-name is the difference between the idealist and the ideologue. The idealist is impelled by what he or she sees as long-term benefits of realistic actions; theirs is more of an inductive approach that adds up to the idealized goal. The ideologue tends to start from the top, as with the syllogism, requiring actions that are considered to fulfill the concept, but the major premise governs regardless of the practicality or benefit of the individual actions that are deduced from it. In other words, the highest level of abstraction of the Structural Differential blinds the ideologue from looking down the ladder to the reality level—the authoritarian mindset is at play.

A major human characteristic is our investment in symbolizing. Symbols are surrogates for things, convenient handles, and words are a prime example. Okay. But we need to ask ourselves what the symbols stand for. An excellent expression of the failure to keep the icon separate from what it represented was given by a tenth-grader waving a Confederate flag at a demonstration. As quoted in a *New York Times* article by Anthony DiPalma (Wednesday, March 13, 1991), the boy said, "My ancestors died for this flag. I believe what it stands for." When asked what it stood for, he said, "I forget."

The Abstraction Level in Science

Science is chock-a-block with concepts, as scientists summarize or categorize their observations. Quite simply, though, these terms for intangibles are rigorously tied to the reality level by definitions that are established by scientific organizations. If there were a dispute as to whether some observation represented one phenomenon or another, statistically valid evidence would have to be brought forth to make the case or the issue would go unresolved.

There are very few abstraction levels between the reality and the concept. A lodestone will attract iron filings, an effect called ferromagnetism, and an electric current in a wire will create a magnetic field around it called electromagnetism. Both terms can be subsumed under "magnetism," but how much higher in abstraction level could one go? Perhaps, "natural force."

Some concepts, such as "causality," may be largely philosophical, and some scientists might share that weighty view with the rest of society. In science as such however, "causality" does not imply some mysterious, unfathomable inspiration as it does in religious terms. "Cause" in science is simply a sequence of events for which the preceding and probable succeeding events are known or at least considered to be knowable. A thing can be called a cause if it continually is present before some succeeding event and where the latter does not occur without the former. Ascribing cause in this way is a rational decision, devoid of any mystical forces.

Abstract ideas in science aren't value-loaded. Radioactivity may be harmful to humans, but it isn't considered evil. It simply exists in dumb innocence as a phenomenon, which can even be beneficial for medical and other uses.

Some concepts may, however, be labels for generalized ideas and do take on values. Think of "environmental pollution," for example. This is a generalized rubric, not a specific concept, as such. To have the status of the latter, one would have to describe what type of pollution, and it would have to be related to sources and amounts—evidence, again. So this subject can be subsumed under higher abstractions of "moral issue," "social issue," or "political issue," etc., where it would be incumbent on those discussing it to give the facts.

Summary

The important actions that people take depend upon the evaluations they have made. What makes some people conservative, some progressive, some punitive, and some forgiving? The factors that contribute to personality are many, complex, and interrelated, and is not the purpose of this book. Nor is it claimed that what has been covered is exhaustive; what the latest studies show would undoubtedly add more insight. The aspects covered are basic and minimal, however. The evaluations we make depend not only on those inputs mentioned at the start of this chapter, but on the substantive ideas we develop. In that process, we will have abstracted similarities from the specifics of situations to lump them into some classification. Likewise, we draw similarities from these classifications to form still higher classifications. At each level, our ideas become less tied to real-life anchors and are rather more abstract. Finally, we come to an idea that is a super-abstraction of the original situation, which is not simply a generalization. As the summation of our reasoning and impressions, it is a concept or belief we firmly hold.

At each level, we sense that certain values are attached. So at the highest level, our confidence in the conclusion we've reached represents a value that is deeply held. Here is where our more conscious, literal thinking melds with our less conscious beliefs that lurk in the sub-basement of our mind. Our basic beliefs, acting as a whole system, affect the substantive ideas we have developed about any subject. As much as it is necessary to zero in on the specifics of our ideas and to be aware of the many inputs as to how we develop them, it is the underlying beliefs, not the substantive ideas, that guide our actions.

It is hard to change one's beliefs, maybe impossible. Still, if we think it's worthwhile or necessary to understand or change opinions—ours or others'—we need to examine beliefs and how they developed over time.

I submit that if we can understand how we evaluate people and situations, we will come to a greater comity between individuals, groups, and nations.

PART IV

A SUPPLEMENT

CHAPTER 13

Statistics:
The Numbers Game

hat would a book that extols the scientific mode of thought be without some mention of math? Mathematics is the language of science. Don't worry. This won't be an excursion into that fearsome territory that so many of us dreaded in school. Something ought to be said, though, about the way we use numbers. They are so obviously useful, but we can be tyrannized by them.

Think how we dread approaching some decade of our age. Being thirty (or forty) isn't much older than twenty-nine (or thirty-nine), yet at thirty-one or forty-one, we can relax until we approach another decade. The advent of the year 2000 seemed to have dramatic significance with forecasts of doom, yet it was a millennium only in an arbitrarily accepted calendar. Talk about frame of reference! Mystical significance has been attributed to numbers through the ages—"unlucky thirteen" is probably the prime example. Numbers often are used to impress, as we consider bigger is better or more terrible. Some people throw numbers around (validly or not), using an abstraction level above reality, to bolster their facts and to impress their listeners or readers.

Yet numbers help us to be specific, as noted in Chapter 2. They help us to pin down qualitative aspects, though this is often done with a facile attempt to seem scientific. For example, applause meters quantify approval, however loosely. People are asked to show agreement or disagreement on a scale of 1 to 10 in questionnaires. A public demonstration can be evaluated by the size of a crowd measured from an aerial photograph. Literary style has even been quantified by elaborate formulae. Numbers help to sharpen qualitative comparisons.

Perhaps the ultimate in a valid technological use of numbers is the way graphic representations, such as sound waves in electronic communication or electrocardiograms, etc., can be digitized. Still, numbers do have validity when used properly. Presenting mere numbers as data can be inadequate or misleading, so it pays to be a bit savvy about how they are combined. I'm referring to statistics.

Don't get nervous! In what follows, I want merely to show that there are quantitative parallels for the qualitative matters discussed in the previous twelve chapters. These analogs are used as a scientific way to make diffuse evaluations more definitive. Statistics as a discipline lets us check the validity of results in any kind of investigation that produces data and helps to reveal trends with relative rigor. The more important practical result is to make valid predictions and cast extra light onto previous discussions about some of these statistical tests. What follows will take you through an echelon of levels for probing the caveats about the outputs and inputs covered so far.

The term "statistics" is used regularly but improperly to mean the numbers themselves that people throw around. The proper use of the term refers to the mathematical techniques for homing in on the validity of data and the way it is obtained. These techniques can be applied to data for any number of purposes: economic or political trends, sociological or psychological studies, scientific experiments—the list goes on and on.

The Role of the Dice

How can one know that conclusions based on data are valid even though the data themselves are reliable? Haven't we all heard that figures don't lie, but liars do figure?

Since we can't check every instance or participant in some large-scale situation, we have to rely on taking a sample. But how representative is the sample? That leads to the next question: Because a sample is not definitive, what is the *probability* that it is adequate and valid?

These questions became compelling around the turn of the twentieth century when the population surged after huge waves of immigrants flooded into the United States. The resulting demographic and social problems placed a huge burden on insurance companies, which had to figure probabilities of life spans, death rates, and so on. Being able to make reliable predictions became imperative, and figuring probabilities was the name of the game. This was actually the origin of the discipline of statistics, when, in the seventeenth century, the mathematics of probability were worked out to determine the role of the roll of the dice. Probability is now the ultimate criterion for evaluating the results of any investigation.

It is one of those ironies of history where trends of thought in different fields come together at the same time that probability played an important part in the development of science. In the mid-1800s, the Second Law of Thermodynamics ("Heat can't flow uphill," that is, from a colder to a hotter body) was shown to depend upon the probability of gas molecules hitting one another. Fifty years later, probability became the basis for quantum mechanics and Heisenberg's Uncertainty Principle.

What follows is only a smattering of the techniques available to statisticians. My purpose is to describe the ways that can be used to check aspects to ensure good evaluations, not to go into the mathematics.

The simplest use of statistics is in presenting ratios or percentages. That's very easy arithmetic, but the choice of numerator and denominator can get sticky because people choose these selectively. An airline, for example, might tout its safety record by noting how many passenger miles it has flown without an accident. Very comforting. But an airline that travels long distances and/or uses very large planes can show a terrific safety record on this basis. Since most accidents occur on take-offs or landings, a more valid and revealing ratio would be to show the number of accidents per flight. Ratios for the state of the national economy or about stock market returns can also be chosen selectively to support a desired viewpoint.

We might read, for example, about "average household income." Such figures are convenient, but minimal and simplistic. They are equivalent to overgeneralizations. How are these averages obtained? If an employer who earns $1,000,000 dollars a year is in a room with ten of his employees, each of whom earns only $20,000 per year, the numerical average salary would be $510,000. We all learned in school that a simple average of the highest and lowest figure is inappropriate, but even the *mean,* calculating the sum of all eleven salaries and dividing by eleven, would give an approximate figure of $109,091. This, too, might be misleading. It doesn't tell us where the bulk of the salaries lie. So we could deal with the *median* (above and below which there is the same number of salaries) or the *mode,* the most frequent figures. While these measures would give an indicative salary amount, they wouldn't indicate how the various salaries were distributed within the range. Statisticians have better indicators, called the *variance* and the *standard deviation. Variance* accounts for the values and number of salaries above and below the mean and their distances from the mean, so it gives, for normal distributions, a more in-depth picture of the values, frequency, and distribution of the salaries within the range. No longer a serving of only soup and dessert, this is the full meal. The variance is a squared number to eliminate the negatives (below the mean) divided by the number of items; when "unsquared," the variance produces the standard deviation represented by the Greek letter sigma. (Note: The example of salaries cited above is not a normal distribution.)

Data are at the lowest level for calculations—like the ground under the basement level—but the *standard deviation* is on the main floor of the statistical structure and is a key to unlocking most other statistical calculations, quantifying the "more or less" of an item. If standard deviation were quoted with what is frequently cited as "averages," a reader would have a more substantial way to evaluate the item. Tolerances on the accuracy of polling data are given, if reported responsibly.

A Map that *is* the Territory

There is a way to graph data so that the probability of the validity of the data can be determined. Statistical evaluations of a particular matter depend upon the strength of observations and the number of times we find each observation. I'm referring here to the observations of the same kind that we make about only one situation. Many readers, for instance, may have gotten mailings from some political candidate who wants to know how his or her constituency feels about a number of different subjects. He or she might send them a questionnaire with each subject listed in a vertical column, and a scale of "Disagree Strongly" to "Agree Strongly" horizontally along the top. For each item, a tally could be made of the number of people who had the various amounts of disagreement or agreement. For each item, we would plot on a horizontal scale a numerical value to each degree of disagreement (negative numbers), with "Don't Know" or "No Opinion" equal to zero, and equivalent numbers for agreement on the positive side. On the vertical scale at each horizontal value, we would plot the number of people in that category. This would give us a *histogram* like most of us drew in arithmetic classes. The diagram may have one major peak or a few minor peaks.

If we took a huge number of observations, a roughly bell-shaped curve would develop in most cases. There is a theoretical calculation that produces this bell curve, called a "normal curve," representing a "normal distribution" (Fig. 14).

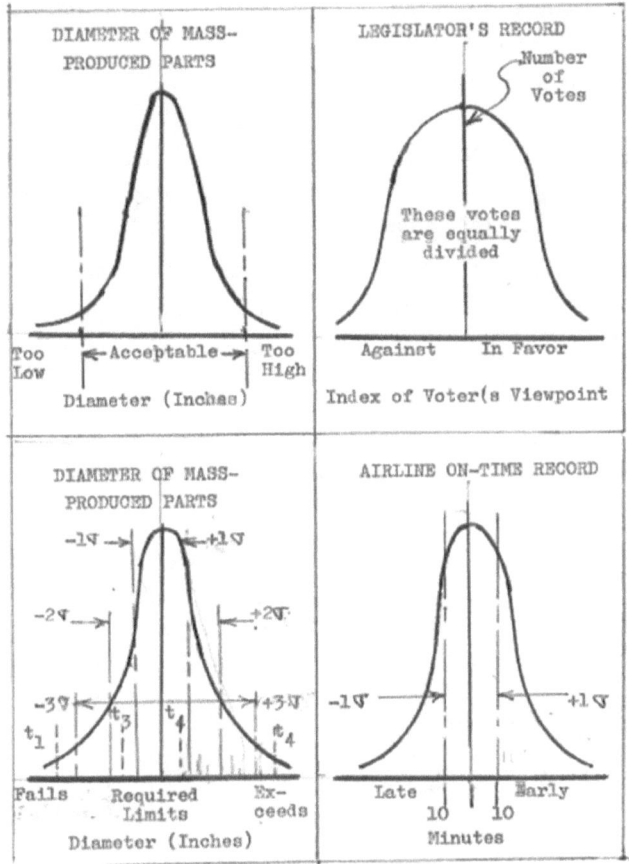

Fig.14. Normal Bell Curves.

The curves are symmetrical to the vertical axes because in such a theoretically large distribution, the values that depart from normalcy (the ones that would show as little mountain peaks on the side of a histogram) are relatively few and have little effect.

The normal curve is the basic map from which statisticians navigate. For a large population of data, pro or con opinions, or values greater than or less than the mean, it gives a pictorial representation of the distribution of these values.

Not all distributions of data are normal, however, so some curves may be non-normal, or "skewed". An example is the height of people depending on age. Once a person reaches maturity, heights are within a narrow range (Fig. 15).

Data falling into either of the two tails of a normal curve depend upon very few items. The chance of some occurrence in either area is rather remote whereas the data for the rest of the map is far more likely. Therefore, this map can be used to determine the probability of something occurring, as will be described later on. Note in Figures 14 and 15, the curve never touches the X-axis. That is because there is always a chance, however remote, that something with a very high or very low value will occur with a very low frequency. This is the equivalent of avoiding the use of the words *always* and *never*.

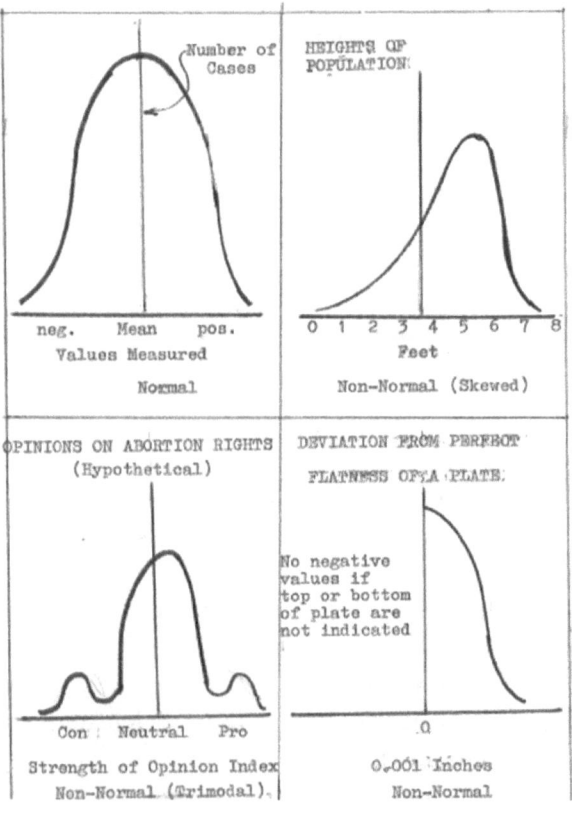

Fig. 15.Normal versus Non-normal (Skewed) Bell Curves.

People expressing a wide range of agreement or disagreement with some statements in a poll may produce a wide curve; if most respondents agreed with a certain behavior, the curve would be relatively narrow. A strongly polarized response may show a narrow, skewed, or irregular curve (Fig. 15).

Bell curves can be drawn for scores calculated from data and for calculations of various sorts. The breadth of a curve reflects the maximum and minimum values of observations made, as well as the variability within those observations (the variance and the standard deviation).

Mathematically, one standard deviation on each side of the mean (taken together) encompasses 68 percent of the data that makes up the distribution (the area under the normal curve), a two sigma variation covers 95 percent, and three sigma covers about 99 percent (Fig. 16).

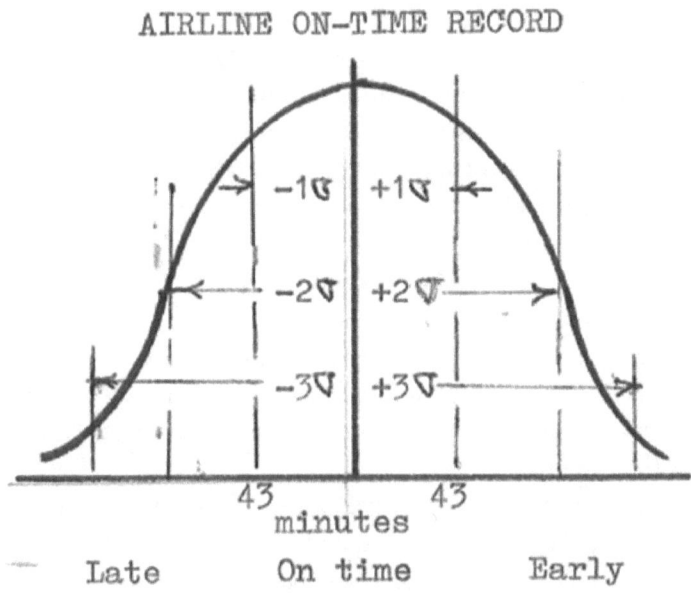

Fig. 16. Standard Deviations (sigmas).

Data occurring within one sigma is like saying, "Some of the time"; if within two sigma, "Much of the time"; and for three sigma, it's equivalent to "Most of the time." If an investigator's data falls within two sigma (on either side of a neutral value), he can say that 95 percent of the data falls within its limits. One way to evaluate different samplings of a particular situation is to compare the standard deviations of each sampling with one another.

The statistician's bag of tricks also includes a mathematical magic wand by which the numerical values for the measurements he took are converted into *scores* (z—or t-scores). This is the next floor up from the main floor sigma. These scores, rather than the raw data, reflect how individual data compares to the group from which it was taken. That is, the scores reflect the frequency of different values, their distribution around the mean, and the standard deviation of the sample.

One example of the usefulness of z-scores is avoiding a faulty comparison that many people make: comparing apples and oranges. This comes up in contentious issues involving people of different races, ethnicities, or socioeconomic classes, as in educational achievement. We might hear that some white students being admitted to college are in the top 10 percent of their class, as are some black students. But is the top 10 percent of an upper-income, mainly white high school equivalent to the upper 10 percent from a lower-income, largely black high school? The z-scores from each group give a fairer comparison. These scores are also used for the next step up: answering the question about the probability of results occurring from valid variables or from random chance.

Because the normal curve is based on theoretically extremely large samples, tables of numbers representing the areas under the curve for one, two, and three sigmas have been worked out. These areas represent the occurrence of data found in those areas and the likelihood of their occurrence. So for a particular score, the table gives the areas under the curve—that is, the probability of its occurrence. This is a major ingredient for the statistician to be able to make an evaluation or to demonstrate a hypothesis that he favors.

To evaluate a given group, however, more care is needed. This occurs in poll-taking. These days, many of us may be asked to answer questionnaires over the phone. Poll results can give a good representation of how we feel about a whole host of things: consumer views, political opinions, and so on. Poll-taking organizations abound, and they can reflect real democracy *if* these organizations are not fronts for groups or companies that have an agenda they wish to promote. By clever wording of questions and selective statistical presentations, they can publicize what they claim is the will of the people.

An unbiased investigation has to answer several questions: How reliable are the data? Were enough samples taken or large enough ones to give a true picture of what the investigator wants to find out? Assessing the sample(s), you can see, is a critical necessity. We tend to value a person's opinion more the wider that person's experience is. How little experience can we trust? Sloppy sampling, or biased data, can skew the results. Statisticians have various tests to answer these questions.

A responsible investigator would take several samples. How consistent they are or how widely they vary is something one would want to know. Figure 17 is meant to illustrate this for two laboratories testing the thickness of gold plating on a sample. Tolerances on the precision of measurement are established by the investigators. There may be differences between samples from Lab No. 2, but also differences between those results and data from Lab. No. 1. Reliance on any one set of samples could bias the true picture.

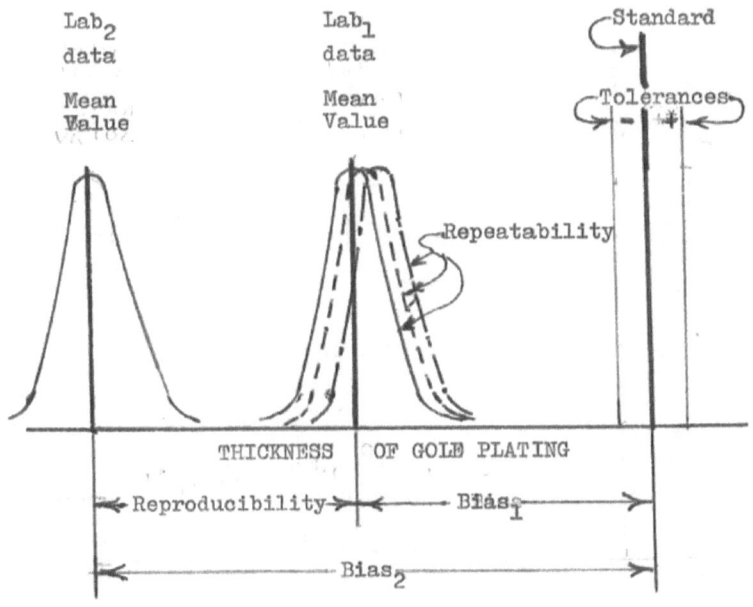

Fig. 17. Variation within and between data sources.

The *standard error of the mean*, that is, the standard deviation of the mean of all the samples, would reflect this. The range of agreement in polls of political opinion, the causes of social problems, or the effectiveness of economic solutions or medical cures—all of these would give an indication of how broad the problem was and what degree of action had to be taken.

Consistency between samplings is only one level of interest. It's one thing to take multiple samples in an area that you feel is homogeneous, but another if some factors enter that might represent non-homogeneity. To find that out, we have to move up one more level in the statistical building.

At that more significant level, the experimenter wants to know about differences between his samples. If some data seem far-fetched, do they still reflect the situation he is checking, or could they be spurious and random, having occurred just by chance? Do the differences between the samples make a difference?

Suppose a bunch of people are talking about one of the subjects mentioned above, and one person offers an opinion that diverges widely from the rest. The participants might say, "You're crazy. That's impossible!" In cases like this, one can't do an instant, thorough scholastic investigation to see how off-base the odd opinion is, even if some in the group may have in-depth knowledge. In some matters, as in the choice of medical opinions if a person went for a second opinion, it could be critical to assess how off the mark the controversial opinion could be.

Statistics can tell how well the samples represent an overall larger population. Techniques can show if the distribution of data from the samples is normal or if some of them don't truly represent the overall population.

What if opinions about a political candidate are being sought from different parts of the country? Several samplings in each part of the country may be consistent enough, but those samplings in the south seem to differ from those in New England or California. How well do these different samples represent the national assessment of the candidate? Are there real differences between the groups that come from different parts of the nation, or are they variables that enter randomly by chance alone?

These questions also apply when the effect of known variables is being sought. It's relatively easy to think about one variable (e.g., different parts of the country) affecting an outcome. The need for understanding isn't that simple, though. In today's complex world, many variables can act at once, and it's important to learn about their effects. So we climb to another level.

Look again at some of the cases mentioned above. Suppose we want to find out which of several methods would be better to use—be they medical treatments, public policies, teaching methods, or others. It's likely that there could be seemingly wide differences between samples representing each method. So again, we have to find out how significant these differences are. Do they truly reflect the different methods, or did they occur by chance? It is very easy for the latter to happen, considering how many things affect a situation, and how an opinion-taker or experimenter has to choose somewhat selectively the limited factors he will investigate. His choices will depend very often upon his frame of reference.

When trying to assess the effect of purposely introduced multiple variables, the same question applies as for unknown variables. That is, do all these samples represent an overall situation where the introduced variables had no effect, or have the different methods in fact made a difference?

Whereas a layman making overblown generalizations might claim that his opinion represents the whole story, the statistician has a way of making a rigorous estimate of the whole situation from the sample(s) taken. This is an inductive problem, where the general conclusion has to depend upon the accumulated individual facts. Sorting out the effects of the relationships between complex variables gets a little tricky for reasons that we need not go into here, but it can be done with statistical rigor, again with a chosen degree of probability.

By running an "analysis of variance" from the different samples, the statistician can determine whether the different samples represent the total picture, or whether differences among the samples, such as the effect of different parts of the country or the use of different teaching methods, had a significant effect.

We are getting near the top of the building, but we still have a way to go before we get to the observation deck for a far-reaching view of a situation.

A Declaration of Independence

So far, the discussion has covered the questions of whether a difference between samples makes a difference and to what extent differences exist that they might represent the effects of some variables. As important as it is to know that, it is the minimum knowledge we need to put methods into effect, and, if possible, to improve situations. Given the effect of some teaching methods, for instance, we need to pin down a few more levels of understanding.

The previous questions discussed are analogous to asking how representative different people's opinions are of some situations. That gives us a static picture of the case. Various sources of these differences were explored in earlier chapters. But what about the dynamic? How independent are the variables of one another? To make sound judgments about that very practical problem, a sophisticated opinion seeker or experimenter needs to get to the bottom of that analysis. Do the different variables act independently? Are the results when one variable is acting alone different if another variable is acting separately by itself at the same time? Are the two variables acting together with some combined effects? Here we get into causes and effects. Are they related? This addresses the *post hoc ergo propter hoc* fallacy.

There's a myth that says, "Women are lousy drivers." If "lousy driving" could be measured in some way, and if data showed this to be reliable information, is it because of the driver's sex or from other factors, e.g., women hadn't taken driver's education or they left most of the driving to the men in the family? Which variable leads to what effect? These kinds of relationships can be assessed by the use of the chi-square function.

Political opinion polling is another good example. Suppose people from the two major political parties, Democrat and Republican, were asked their opinions on, say, abortion rights. It could be easy for an uninformed person to make a judgment about what stand the adherents of one party or the other might take.

Here is where the reader of "what the latest studies show" may be in the dark as to how well those studies were done, for the chi-square technique requires that pairs of the presumed factors also have to be measured. As to women drivers, for instance, driving habits would have to be observed for both good and bad examples, and for each, women would have to be compared with men. For the political matter, Democrats and Republicans would each have to be questioned about their pro-abortion and anti-abortion stances.

Forming Lasting Relationships

Suppose we find that variable A leads to effect B in a particular test. Is this relationship consistent for other instances? If it is, we ought to be able to know something about an individual from the information about the group as well as the reverse. Up to this point, we have only discussed how we could learn about an overall group or situation from a sample. Establishing a two-way relationship would be more reliable than simply depending upon stereotypes or labeling someone based upon the group he belongs to.

A popular opinion is that crime is often related to race or ethnicity. It's too easy to make this claim from highly visible, anecdotal reports or those in the news media. But is a high crime rate *because* of ethnicity or is the connection merely apparent? Might it not be related to economic or social factors like poor education or low self-esteem?

Bear in mind that to show a relationship does not mean necessarily that this is a cause-and-effect case. Two characteristics may coexist while some other factor is the actual cause. So a person has to be on solid ground in assuming that if characteristic A exists, B may exist also, even if one doesn't cause the other. Personality factors are a case in point: One's outlook on a political matter may coexist with a tendency to dogmatism, but neither *causes* the other. This might guide our expectations about one's political orientation on various issues. The strength of the relationship can be evaluated as a buffer against a layman's going from an unwarranted assumption to a foregone conclusion. For this evaluation, the statistician uses "regression analysis," which will establish if a relationship exists. (Fig.18). A plot of data matching factor A on the vertical scale against B on the horizontal scale might show a lot of scatter, even though a trend would be apparent

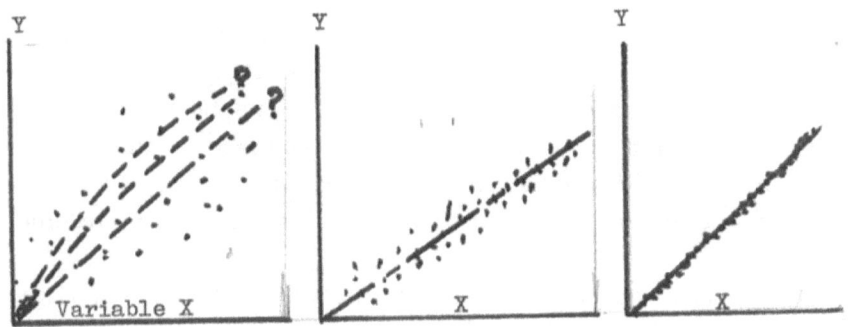

Fig.18. Regression curves showing degrees of correlation.

But how close is the relationship? Can we use it to make predictions? That, after all, is the ultimate, practical goal of any investigation, and it is the ultimate, practical outcome of our opinion-forming. But it has to be done reliably. If there is a lot of scatter, we would not know where to draw the proper curve. Judging by eye would be a poor indicator to make a prediction.

The more data we plotted, the closer we could come to drawing a curve from the points. Such a curve would show the extent to which A and B depended upon each other. If there were a consistent curve, we could extend it to predict the relationship at higher values than those plotted.

If the curve were a straight line, we would get a simple arithmetic relationship. Also, the slope of the line would show the extent to which A or B affect each other. Still, this would be only a general trend (Fig.18); we would still want to know how close the dependency was. This can be calculated as a "correlation factor." This is like honing accuracy to give us precision. We are now just about at the top of the statistical edifice.

A low correlation value would indicate a poor correlation (Fig. 18a). A correlation factor of 0.5, for example, would mean that the two factors relate to each other fairly well (Fig. 18b). The best correlation factor is 1.0, meaning that all points would fall on a straight line (Fig. 18c). A change in the independent variable would always lead to a known change in the dependent variable. If only things in life were that simple and predictable!

Finally, an experimenter wants to have confidence in his results, and he needs a way to answer the degree of confidence. This is the last upward step for all practical purposes. It amounts to asking someone, "How confident are you that you have all your facts straight on which you're basing your opinion?" It puts limits on the likelihood of extreme values that someone might spout for dramatic effect. The selective use of data that are found in stereotypes or used by bigots is avoided by this technique of statistics.

Since very few occurrences fall into the tails of the bell curve, these areas are used to check the probability of whether or not observations represented by these points come from experimental factors. So an experimenter can claim, for instance, that his results are "significant at the .01 level," that is, there is less than one chance out of a hundred that the results came purely from chance; and there is a 99 percent probability that his results truly come from the experimental variables. Statistical formulations lead to calculation of probability for the data. These can be plotted against the frequency of the observations (Fig. 19)

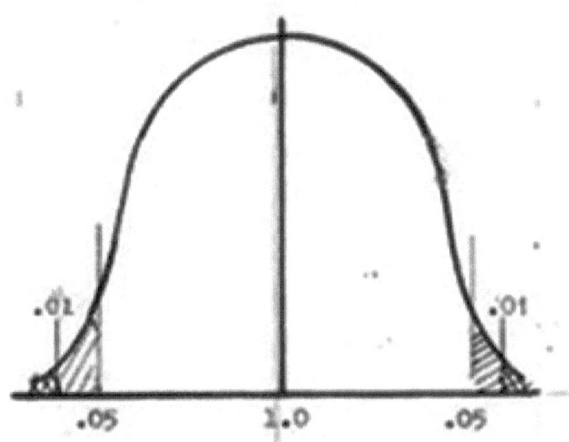

Fig. 19. Probability that results occurred by chance.

Results for which probability calculations fall within "significance levels" (shaded zones) customarily chosen are considered to have come from experimental manipulation of variables rather than from chance alone.

Whatever technique the statistician is using, be it analysis of variance or chi-square, for example, determining the significance level of the results—the probability of their occurrence by chance or because of known factors—is the statistician's proving ground for his mathematical arsenal.

Summary

I now will review how the various statistical tools mentioned above are mathematical analogs for the outputs and inputs of evaluation dealt with in earlier chapters. Overall, the awareness of uncertainty and the avoidance of dogmatism are represented by the basic concept of probability. Relativism is accounted for by viewing samples in the context of an overall population and in techniques for comparing samples. Being specific is answered by numerical data as well as in the way results of various tests are stated. Generalizing is made solid and stereotyping is avoided by getting a picture, with determined probability and significance of how samples and overall population are related. Either/or evaluations are avoided because data that lands in the tails of normal distribution curves represent only contraries of a continuum, not contradictories. Frames of reference and selective perception are reflected in analyses of how consistent samples are with one another, how well they represent a larger group, and by assessing the effect of different variables.

Do you see how all these statistical tools of the trade are inductive in nature? They all build up a conclusion about validity or probability of a conclusion or hypotheses from individual data. An experimenter may start out with a hypothesis he or she hopes to demonstrate, but that is only the goal; it guides the procedure he or she will follow but doesn't determine it dogmatically. The proof is in the data that develops. Probability, significance levels, and poor correlations, to cite a few examples, could shoot down any premises that might have been based on unrealistic abstractions.

This chapter is meant to show only some of the mathematical tools that statisticians use to reach a reliable evaluation. The average person can't be expected to be even minimally educated about statistics, and that field gets more and more complicated and specialized. Despite the rigor of the math, however, statisticians may err, even if the person or group touting the figures isn't trying to obfuscate.

Most analyses assume a normal distribution. But if an analysis is made on this assumption when a distribution is not normal, even though there are techniques for making proper comparisons, the conclusions drawn will be misleading. An investigator might claim similarity between groups where none existed; he might neglect to do or to report an analysis of variance, thus misreading the effect of a variable. A straight-line correlation might be claimed based on a graphical presentation of data, however irresponsibly, rather than on a calculated correlation factor. The degree of significance, an arbitrary choice even though there are standard practices, might be fudged so as to claim some conclusion is very good when it is only passably so. All sorts of corners might be cut for various careless, practical, or unethical reasons.

My hope is that you have become a little more alert and more savvy (and not more cynical) about the information in this chapter.

Epilogue

C hapter 13 on statistics was meant to demonstrate that the way scientists think is not a random process, but is one that follows a sequence of increasingly discrete steps, all grounded on the basic and minimum requirements of evidence and measurement. The individual techniques trace the concepts that science (if not always individual scientists) presents as a model for making sound, unbiased evaluations. The process is one of trying to reach conclusions inductively from the bottom up, instead of starting from the top down with random, loosely examined, abstract assumptions. Alternative interpretations and explanations need to be sought, as dogmatic and ideological positions run counter to the way science operates.

Above all, I hope that you have become aware that attitude plays a part in being able to think smart and talk smart. You have been encouraged to be self-analytical and open-minded, but these states of mind require honesty and diligence. It is my hope, however idealized, that the principles outlined here and the attitudes referred to can become more widespread. Thus, many sources of misevaluation would disappear, and our problems at the personal, group, or international level might be more readily and effectively approached.

ADDENDUM to First Edition

When Oscar Wilde's first book did not sell very well, he took out an ad in a local newspaper saying that due to the popularity of the book, he had it reissued as a "Second Edition" That supposed popularity caused the book to sell like hot cakes. The re-issue of this book with this chapter does not make it technically a Second Edition, due to publishing rules; but this version is not for publicity. It has a sober, practical motivation. Since effective communication involves getting through to someone with an exchange of ideas rather than simply getting to them, this addendum will amplify some of the principles discussed in the first edition, with added thoughts about relevant issues.

The hectic world we live in today seems to involve an increasing pace of technical progress that is almost too much for humans to be able to manage; but humanity has been through such changes before. If we are unaware of history we may see ourselves in the worst (or best) light; but people in earlier centuries have been through all the same kinds of turmoil and responses before. We may think of Gutenberg's printing press as simply an antique turning point in history, yet its rapid rise of book publishing and the wide-spreading knowledge that ensued led to a marked opening of people's minds Newton and Galileo brought about other leaps in human understanding of the physical world, as did Luther's unleashing of Protestantism and Darwin's shaking up of man's understanding of his origins in the realm of thought. The advent of the steam engine meant that the typical labor in the out of doors with farming gave way rapidly to indoor repetitive work in noisy, crowded factories, often sweat shops (not to mention an order of magnitude change in the production of carbonaceous gases into the atmosphere). Yet humans overcame these stresses, just as today we are finding ways to relieve our burdens by developing robots.

In the not-too-distant future, when nations will probably be contending with each other in space, down here on Earth we will need to be more universally managed. Control of population, and of land, sea and air as well as of natural resources will be a practical necessity. A world government will be needed; and it can be put into effect with the aid of computerized algorithms. Historical development and practical necessity all point to this.

These trends make it all the more important that we understand the events surrounding us, that we communicate very clearly with our fellow citizens and our legislators, and that we develop leaders whose intellectual probity trumps ego or political position.

In the six years since the first edition of this book was published, new trends have taken hold which have altered---or attempt to do so—our social outlook. We are increasingly swamped with information. There is an excrescence of verbiage. Clever services are offered endlessly on the internet. A multitude of electronic devices have become venues to satisfy the voracious appetite of advertisers who intrude on unwary viewers.

Social media have provided more opportunities than ever for incorrect misinterpretations, even outright lies. The latter may be, as usual, for political purposes or to press an extreme view point. The old-fashioned propaganda techniques have given way to instantaneous inoculations with treacherous viruses. Some of the "alternative facts" may be malevolently disseminated: It is ironic, but we might have expected that cynical internet operators would set up sites to disseminate spectacular but fabricated "news" with the aim of attracting advertisers' money because of the artificially produced wide audience. Hackers with increasing sophistication interfere with individuals, corporations and governments. This may even be criminal.

Wilde's fake news was a clever ploy but harmless, when compared with these up-dated types of "news." In earlier centuries rumors could be spread by word of mouth to the detriment of vulnerable individuals or a credulous populace with devastating results. Today's internet with the instantaneity, the world-wide pervasiveness and the explosion of information, sadly, exacerbates that human failing. If Moore's "law" holds, we can expect a geometric increase in the capabilities of computers to affect this dynamic.

On the positive side, clever and sophisticated digital innovators continually try to set up programs that will supplant human evaluations. They try to "train" computers to recognize hate speech, political biases and so on. The ultimate goal is to develop robots that can think and evaluate like humans on any subject. No matter how close to human thoughts these programs may be, the effort would seem to have no end-point in the infinite combinations of human ideas. The effort becomes regressive; for, as with the fallacy of the Ontological argument purported to prove the existence of God, it is always humans who are designing the programs.

Now we have the advent of self-driving cars. The teams of experts who design the circuits to foresee and prevent the kinds of contingencies that human error could encounter will all have been trained to think like scientists. But that does not let us off the hook. We have to guard against their automation from lulling us into abdicating our own judgment in this or any other case.

How can one separate fact from fiction? One might trust a monitoring organization that claims to be non-partisan, but the problem regresses: how can a person be sure of that? So ultimately this gets down to how astutely a person makes the judgement. Thus it behooves us more strongly than ever to develop acuity and objectivity: to think like a scientist.

As noted earlier, starting with William James towards the end of the 19th century, the basic modes of psychology have been enunciated. Personality aspects have been explained by Freud, Erikson and others. Interrelationshjps have been described by Carl Rogers, Anatol Rappaport *et al.* So it is now the grist of infinite human behaviors, taken two or more at a time, that are being investigated by PhD. candidates. The forefront of research in human behavior is increasingly being analyzed by neuroscientists. They are aided by constantly refined devices such as the M.R.I. This discipline gets below the practical level of purely personal discourse to find the sources of behaviors in the brain. Yet in revealing where some mental activities are located this is still only one level of explanation below that of what "common sense" might point to. Motivations, agendas, predilections will still exist.

Recently, cognitive scientists, at least, have come to realize that their own work is subject to the Quantum Physics tenet that the observer affects the observed. Researchers have become sensitive to the way their choice of parameters is not only based on a grab-bag of technical matters, however appropriate; but their personalities, body language and demeanor may be affecting the responses of their clients. What people often sense in the demeanor of someone they are having a discussion with (the "vibes" they get) has been given a worthy and necessary refinement in accord with the scientific way of communicating.

Basic criteria of the scientist's thinking style

I distinguish between the scientists' style of thinking and science, as such. For while scientists are trained in this mode of thinking, it does not apply only to making science; it should be used in making decisions or evaluations for all aspects of life just as it does for non-scientists.

The scientist's thinking style described in the first edition can be summed up into these basic points: (1) open-mindedness. (2) relying only on reproducible evidence;(3) thinking inductively,(4) abjuring metaphysical thinking;(5) freedom from dogmatism;(6)overcoming rigidity; (7) developing principles from reliable facts,(8) not choosing evidence selectively to fit ${}_a prioi$ principles[7]. (9) taking a holistic approach; (10) thinking operationally; (11) defining standards and terminology functionally, (12) finally, balancing opposites.

Many of these points may seem obvious. What differentiates the scientists's style from that of an ordinary intelligent person is that these steps are a recipe for a full meal. It is the totality of these concepts, working together at the same time, that make the way scientists think the paragon of making evaluations and reaching conclusions.

The Plan of Attack

A dynamic is operating with all of these; it involves seeking alternatives, opposites and negatives. Each should be applied to causes and effects, action versus inaction, progress versus stasis and so on. Such thinking may be normal where financial matters (e.g. purchasing stocks, homes, cars) are involved; but that dynamic too often is ignored in other matters. Politicians and legislators often, not thinking likes scientists don't even ask themselves those types of questions.

This dynamic includes seeking a balance between the factors. That necessarily involves ratios.

. One cannot determine effectively what is right or what is wrong in a situation; such judgements are too subjective and non-measurable.

---

[7]   Established principles obviously can be used to guide actions, as long as the latter are consistent with the principles.

Instead, what should be considered is benefit versus loss. This ratio will depend, of course, on the agendas of the participants. Such a ratio lends itself to statistical examination of evidence presented to support a position. How we assess risk and benefit is the major theme in the

best-selling book, "Thinking Fast and Slow," by the Nobel laureate, Daniel Kahneman.

He discusses the dynamics of risk-taking in detail. The simplest type of bet involves heads versus tails; typically, what will A get if B does so and so. More usual, however, is a situation like this:

What will A do if B does so and so *in view of* situation C, or even situations C and D[8]. Those are the kinds of situations that are involved in much decision-making, certainly in planning scientific ventures, foreign policy outlooks and corporate profit making; they also enter family situations, even though the people involved don't consider all the ifs, ands and buts that linger importantly, undiscerned, in the background.

The author also considers the type of risk that comes from perplexing choices; for ex., where there may be great rewards but with little chance of coming about, versus getting smaller rewards but with greater probability. So on that level, too, applying the aspects of scientific probity is vital.

Listening

Those perceptual aspects described in Chapter 8 refer primarily to visual perception; but they have analogues in audible reception also. Listening is most important. While visually observed situations may be temporal, as in the case of an accident, what is spoken may be more ephemeral. Recordings may have technical inaccuracies, but even if those are not present, what is spoken will still be subject to misinterpretation. Responses to what is said, perhaps in jest, may be misinterpreted, with dire results to ending friendships or provoking severe retaliation. Among these, selective attention is paramount. Responding to speech is apt to be more emotional than responding to something seen. The steps we go through in hearing were given in Chap.9, and the misinterpretations we may make

---

[8] in the 17th century, Blaise pascal worked on the basic mathematics of probability. In the 18th century, Bayes developed formulae for probability where contingent factors had to be considered.

were noted. These are often emotional responses. That critical aspect was elaborated upon by Daniel Kahneman in his book mentioned above. He explains that emotional reactions are instinctive, whereas rational reactions require a pause. Rational assessments require more energy of the brain than do emotional ones.

Kahneman coins an acronym, WYSIATTI (what you see is all there is). That type of response is simplistic, leads to over-generalizations, stereotypes and other misinterpretations. The scientific approach avoids the emotional response to what is heard. This expresses not merely an attitude of interest in a subject but of conditioned attentiveness and curiosity.

Polarities

Gender was alluded to in Chap. 5 but deserves some added thoughts. It is the quintessential characteristic that embodies polarity; and, as if obvious observation were not enough, it is sanctified by the Bible, "Male and female created He them." Also, homosexuality and cross-dressing are forbidden.

As homosexuality (that is, "same-", not simply "male"} came to the public as a situation to be discussed openly, L and G were added to the abbreviations. But there are alternatives: it was acknowledged that it was not either/or but could be both/and, with the addition of bi-sexuality. More recently, those further groups in the shadows of public acknowledgement, trans-genders and transsexuals have been added. A final Q is now often used, standing for "questioning". That acknowledges in very human terms the uncertainty and psychological pain that transgender people may have. Despite the dogmatic refusal of some people, mostly because of religious views, to accept this range of possibilities, open-mindedness has begun to prevail.

The pinnacle of these matters came with the push for gay marriage. For millennia, marriage was thought to mean the joining of (only) a man and a woman in a union legitimized by some authority, religious or governmental---even ship Captains. This bi-gender union had been accepted for millennia, sanctioned by that standard of morality, the Bible, and codified in dictionaries. But dictionaries, issued centuries after the Bible, merely stated the existential reality.

This is a classic example of a layman's dogmatism---the inability to accept new facts----and rigidity---the inability to discern the factors in a situation. The scientific style open-mindedly realizes that apart from cultural tolerance, even with gender, other possibilities might exist. It would recognize the myriad different sex behaviors of all species, and the manifold range of customs among various cultures through the ages. It would point out that the oft-stated purpose of marriage---procreation--- did not hold; for many married couples did not have children, unmarried couples did.

The science-minded view would apply an operational definition: it would have asked," What is the basic function of marriage?"; and it would have answered : to form a bond between any two people who love each other and want to care for each other.

Such an outlook would lead to the acceptance of lesbians, gays, bisexuals and trans-genders as natural, if anomalous, realities.

"Political correctness"

This still-defied pattern is relevant here. Apart from it being a cultural nicety, it reflects a three-step mental process: first, recognizing the source of a characterization; second, being aware of the possibly invidious nature of stating one's subjective impressions outright; finally, seeking alternative words to characterize the object. "P.c." does not mean acceding to the politics of the moment. It acknowledges the expunging of distasteful or harmful outmoded conventional biases from the way we think and talk. This objective mini-calculation is akin to what the scientific thinking style would produce. One might even hold that if this way of "biting one's tongue" before making an intemperate or distasteful remark were to become a normal kind of response that would mark a tiny but worthwhile advance in our civilization.

Relativism

Relativism is a way of evaluating situations. People who do not normally think relativisticly unthinkingly accept a mistaken idea of it. That is, that relativism implies that all values are equal. That flies in the face of moral precepts, especially for people who hold a dogmatic view of their own value system. That is true of conservatives, who almost by definition maintain a dogmatic view. They mis-characterize relativism for political purposes.

The scientific thinking style points to the correct interpretation. That is, that relativism means that in considering your own views one should seek and assess the views of others for comparison. That is a rhetorical analog to Einstein's Theory of Relativity, which holds that stellar bodies have no unique isolated location in Space, but can be located by comparison with another body. This involves making two levels of comparison: one is to see a situation in its present context, and the other is to see it in a similar but different context. : This would be the case for people made tense by the frenetic pace of electronically supplied information noted earlier. The present context would be to consider the current state of technology; the comparative case would be that of the advent of the steam engine and factory life.

Just as cause and effect must each be seen relative to each other, so it ought to be for matters that occupy our daily news. For ex., comparisons are often made between the United States and other countries. Where social matters are concerned, the U.S. may fare better or worse than other nations; in that case, the cultural history should be considered. In situations where numbers are involved, as with finance, factors such as tax rates, trade balances, gross domestic product, the relative geographical and population size may need to be drawn into the equation.

Abortion

Abortion, a vexatious issue, can be examined with a scientific thinking style. Patently, it is not an issue about lower animals, but of humans; so this involves moral and ethical considerations. Those opposed to abortion take a dogmatic position; and so do those in favor of abortion. Those opposed speak of "the rights of the fetus" those in favor speak of women's rights. Thus the two positions are not really comparable: the former is conjectural and spiritual, the latter is existential and pragmatic. The former poses "rights" to an un-matured entity, the latter cites existent rights to a fully matured person. So relativism applies here, with each position being compared to its own context as well as to the other's. This is also a legitimate either/or situation: the woman has an abortion or she doesn't; she can't be a little bit pregnant.

The anti-abortion people call themselves "pro-life" But one cannot stop there; that is not a holistic view. It would be a dead end in thinking. Analyzing more deeply leads to asking what is meant by "life". The pro-life people seem to concentrate on two aspects: the physiological aspects of the fetus; and secondly, it's potential. But potential is not reality; it is an intellectual concept, however powerful.

That predicted potential has to consider the realities of the benefits and risks involved. These include the potential mother's anguish if she has an abortion or equally if she failed to have one; Prohibiting abortion can lead to problems for the child becoming an adult feeling unwanted by a parent, being shunted around between orphan homes or surrogate parents and various distressful psychological problems. There is the inevitable chance of back-alley places for secretive operations that pose dangers for the woman. On the choice side, a woman who has an abortion may have a lingering regret about what her child might have been. The pro-life adherents may save a soul, the pro-choice group save the woman's individuality. It must be admitted that the concept of soul is an abstraction; however deeply felt, it is not subject to evidence or measurement.

Without meaning to take sides in the issue, it is worth noting an inconsistency in the pro-life position. It is almost universally accepted that abortion in the case of rape should be acceptable. But if the fetus is considered that sacred, should it not be saved even after rape? Some pro-life people say that it should. This seems to be an example of Goedel's theorem: if the fetus is discarded, then the pro-life position is not complete; but if the rape victim does not have an abortion, the social stance of the pro-life group regarding rape as a crime would be compromised and thus be incomplete. These are questions that need to be posed and considered in a relativistic manner.

Rationality

Rationality is the sine qua non of the scientific way of thinking; and it is the assumed or presumed mental state of the readers of this book. It is recognized that very many people do not share this outlook. There are many reasons for this, of course. One fundamental reason is the failure of our educational system to inculcate rational modes from the earliest, even pre-school grades. Other reasons come from family upbringing and the influence of clergy or other authority figures. Open-mindedness requires self-awareness and honesty with oneself.

Cause and affect

These coupled aspects are probably the most significant to consider because they represent the basic way life operates. It is usual to hear people complain about a situation and let the complaint linger in the air as if its strength will somehow generate a response. Too often, however, the complainer does not ask what the reason for his claim is. As a result, causes go unsought and problems remain without even an attempt at a solution. Just as every physical action produces a reaction, so in non-material actions a reaction is at least implied; you can't have one without the other.

Closure may be preemptory or incorrect, of course. People tend to offer their own nostrums as causes, based on their frames of reference or biases. The scientific mind-set would be inclined to immediately try to fathom what the cause(s) of the problem might be; and that would imply that at least the germ of a possible solution was being sought.

The pairing of cause with effect invokes the concepts of relativism and of polarity, and the afore-mentioned advice to consider the negative alternatives.

A notable example of these failings came with investigations by a psychologist named Arthur Jensen. He conducted research that showed that African-Americans overall had lower I. Q.'s than the general population. Jensen had long felt that there were genetic bases for behaviors. Arguably, his personal predilections `a priori biases, assumptions?) led to taking his results as an end-point. But this was not closure from a sociological standpoint. His results justified the beliefs of like-minded people, and they arguably put a damper on further investigations as to other causes for the I Q discrepancies. The research begged the question: what other causes for these results other than genetics could there be? As with the relationship between ethnicity and crime brought up in Chap.13, the possibility that poverty-related poor education, self-adopted low self-esteem of a minority culture, etc. could be the causes were not considered.

This seems to be a case where the investigator's personal convictions trumped the full application of the scientist's thinking style. It is like the investigator described in Chap. 7, whose classic interpretation of Mayan "corn stalk" hieroglyphs was overturned 180 degrees. Even scientists, being human, are not immune to being mesmerized by their favored hypothesis.

It is these human fallibilities, which can be dominating, persistent and insidious, that this book has aimed to prevent or overcome. An ultimate goal is implicit in all of these ideas. that is, to solve society's problems wisely and effectively. That would mean that ignorance and narrow vision on the part of lay people and political leaders, at least. would not be perpetuated from one generation to another and would disappear from the way humans made their evaluations. In that idealized world, everyone would think smart and talk smart in the way the ideal scientist is taught to do.

www.ingramcontent.com/pod-product-compliance
Lightning Source LLC
Chambersburg PA
CBHW061248280526
45784CB00002B/677